W9-ATL-792

EVANGELICAL CHRISTIANS AND
THE JEWISH COMMUNITY...

THE
ZION
CONNECTION

DESTROYING THE MYTHS
FORGING AN ALLIANCE

ELWOOD McQUAID

HARVEST HOUSE PUBLISHERS
Eugene, Oregon 97402

Scripture quotations are taken from The New Scofield Study Bible, Copyright © 1967 by Oxford University Press, Inc.

THE ZION CONNECTION

Copyright © 1996 by Harvest House Publishers
Eugene, Oregon 97402

Library of Congress Cataloging-in-Publication Data

McQuaid, Elwood.
    The Zion Connection / Elwood McQuaid.
        p.   cm.
    Includes bibliographical references.
    ISBN 1-56507-449-1 (alk. paper)
    1. Evangelicalism—Relations—Judaism. 2. Judaism—
Relations—Evangelicalism. I.   Title.
BR1641.J83M38   1996
261.2'6—dc20   95-43853
                                                                    CIP

Printed in the United States of America.
96 97 98 99 00 01 / BC / 10 9 8 7 6 5 4 3 2 1

Acknowledgments

My special thanks to Dolores Banse and Sonja Bickings for ably assisting with research for this book, and to Amy Julian, who was responsible for preliminary editing and manuscript preparation.

I am also deeply grateful to a host of friends in the evangelical and Jewish communities who gave their time and energies to advise on and contribute to this volume.

It is my hope that a favorable response from our readers will amply reward all who were willing to unselfishly participate in the project.

Israel has only two solid friends in the world... certain evangelical Christians and some of our own people.
—Menachem Begin, Washington D.C.

Contents

A New Reality

This book is not a plea for a new ecumenicity.

A few decades ago, certain segments of the Jewish community attempted an alliance with mainline Protestant denominations that were committed to a liberal theological and political agenda. The union seemed to center in a kind of spirit of human brotherhood, uncluttered by serious commitments to the Word of God or the God who authored our Bible. But as the winds of hostility against Zionism and Israel stiffened, the alliance began to cool. It seemed that among mainline Protestants, dispensing the spirit of human brotherhood was a selective matter. Protestants holding liberal persuasions in matters of faith invariably find themselves leaning far to the left when political issues are on the table.

A prime example surfaced in 1975, when the United Nations voted its infamous resolution equating Zionism with racism. After an initial pass on the resolution, the National Council of Churches supported the U.N.'s position. This was not surprising in view of the National Council's track record of supporting the world's foremost radicals and their causes. This action (along with many others) exposed such ecumenicity as a body without a soul.

Today, with the seventies far behind us and liberalism increasingly discredited, there has been a definite shift in the wind. For both Jewish and Gentile Americans who have seen the Judeo-Christian foundation upon which their country was built now badly shaken, a new reality has set in. Much to the chagrin of liberal politicians and secular media spin artists, conservatism seems to be thrusting its way up from the grass roots. While analysts try to identify the main personalities behind this phenomenon, I am convinced that we are not seeing a normal political mood swing. People are thinking beyond the limits formerly set for them by others and are deciding what they want life to be for themselves and for the generations to whom the torch will be passed. In other words, it is a time when millions of Americans are going through a radical reassessment process—a reassessment based on street-level realities rather than ideologies spun in Ivy League think tanks.

There are few areas where this process is more obvious than in the developing relations between the growing number of politically conservative Jews and evangelical Christians. Here it seems that the old taboos and shibboleths no longer seem or sound quite right.

A highly visible rift surfaced between politically conservative and liberal Jews when, on June 9, 1994, the Anti-Defamation League issued a report titled "The Religious Right: The Assault on Tolerance & Pluralism in America." On August 2, 1994, 75 prominent members of the national Jewish community sponsored an ad in *The New York Times* condemning the ADL for attacking the Religious Right. The text of the ad, sponsored by Toward Tradition (a group led by Rabbi Daniel Lapin), included this statement:

> Moreover, Judaism is not, as the ADL seems to suggest, coexistent with liberalism. Nor, we wish to emphasize, does the Jewish community speak with one voice on the religious and moral—and political—issues of our

time. Above all, on the issue with which this community does speak with one voice, namely, the survival of Israel, the Jews have no better friends than Evangelical Christians.

For me the episode served as a catalyst. I believe the time has come to speak definitively from the evangelical point of view on matters related to the burgeoning Jewish-evangelical alliance. My intent is not to resuscitate the old ecumenical movement. Quite the contrary: This book is about *understanding*. Who are those evangelicals the late Menachem Begin commended as "solid friends" of Israel? What, after all, are they attempting to achieve— what is their agenda? Can they be trusted as unqualified friends of Israel and the Jewish people?

Ours is a time when evangelicals must develop a better understanding of the Jewish people and why they have historically had such distrust for Christians. Evangelicals must also understand that while the wheels of anti-Semitism continue to grind across the face of the planet, if Jews are in the crosshairs, evangelicals are also marked as undesirables by an increasingly radicalized society. In the intense religious, political, and cultural free-for-all in which we are now engaged, Israel and Jewry may well represent a sort of first line of defense for Bible-believing Christians. It is a matter of urgent mutual interest that we nurture the fragile alliance that has begun to develop.

1

Perceptions

Proselytize is a word that freezes the minds of the great majority of Jewish people and causes certain guardians of Judaism to go into a frenzy. Given the long history of persecution that Jews have endured while among those who have called themselves Christians, we can well appreciate their concern. The idea seems to be that Christians live by a scorekeeping credo that demands delivering souls to their particular sect. Therefore evangelistic efforts by believers in Jesus are seen as little more than scalp-hunting expeditions fueled by a "my kingdom for a convert" obsession. Yet today's evangelicals have great difficulty understanding why such a concept exists or why their desire to share their faith often provokes such volatile responses from their Jewish friends.

Forced conversions, material inducements to change religion, salvation through subterfuge, or coming as undercover agents in the guise of Judaism are tactics far from the hearts and minds of the overwhelming majority of grassroots evangelicals. In fact—and certainly to our shame—the majority of Christians, evangelical or otherwise, have little understanding of the background of anti-Semitism, which is responsible for the prevailing Jewish attitude toward Christianity. Christians, for example, find it difficult to believe that many Jewish people throw everyone deemed "Christian" into the same black pot, where there are no distinguishing features. Catholics or Protestants, evangelicals or liberals, media con men or cultists—it makes no difference. A Christian is a Christian is a Christian.

"I Hated Them All"

Frankly, many sincere Christians are taken aback when they hear how they are perceived by many Jewish people. Let me give a vivid example of such a perception. Several years ago, while on an EL AL flight bound for Tel Aviv, I met a Jewish businessman from California. He had overheard a conversation I was enjoying with a Jewish couple from New York who were on their way to Israel for the first time.

"You'd make a wonderful salesman for Israel," he said with a smile. "In fact, if I had anything to do with the Israeli government, I think I would hire you to just go around talking to people about the country."

After a lengthy discussion about why each of us was making the journey, he posed a question: "You don't look Jewish to me. Are you a Jew?"

"No," I replied, "but I like to think I have a heart for the Jewish people and Israel."

"But I understood you to say that you're going to Israel to write a book about a Jew."

"That's correct," I answered. "He's a Holocaust survivor from Poland."

The businessman was curious. "Why, if you're not Jewish, are you writing a book about a Jew?"

"There's a very simple answer to that question," I responded. "One day I met a Jew who changed my life. Since I met Him, I have never been the same. Consequently, I feel I owe a great debt of gratitude to the Jewish people, so I write books about Israel and Jews."

"Would you mind if I asked another question?" he said.

"Not at all."

"Who is he?"

"Jesus Christ," I responded.

A very serious expression swept the businessman's face. "Could I talk to you for a few more minutes?" he asked.

"Certainly," I replied.

As we sat together, he told a story much like what I have heard from many Jewish people over the years.

"I was reared in Canada," he began. "We were the only Jewish family in a little town, so I was the only Jewish kid in the school. Everyone else in our community was a Christian. Do you know what the favorite pastime of the boys in my school was? Chasing me home from school in the afternoon, calling me a 'Christ killer.' When they were able to catch me, they beat up on me. If I was too fast for them on any given day, they settled for heaving stones at me.

"I can't tell you how many times I ran into our kitchen in tears to ask my mother what I had done to kill Christ. She was never able to give me a satisfactory answer. Although the reason for my being called a 'Christ killer' remained an open question, I had learned one thing very well: I hated them all, and everything they stood for."

This man, from childhood until the day I met him, apparently viewed non-Jews not only as collectively

Christians but as entrenched enemies of his Jewishness as well. Add to this unfortunate perception the idea that such Christians are predatory scalp–hunters who are systematically attempting to obliterate Judaism and destroy Jewish identity, and we can readily understand the resentment and hostility manifested by many Jews toward Christians. Thus such words as *conversion* and the dreaded *proselytize* became shibboleths by which Christians and their organizations are judged and deemed *friend* or *foe*. Those allowed into the *friend* category come with white flag in hand, pronouncing themselves free from the taint of subversive urges to convert Jewish people to faith in Christ. *Foes* are those who openly admit that, as Christian believers, they are under an obligation to "make Him known" (an issue we will discuss later in this book) and consequently are marked as a clear and present danger to all Jews and are to be avoided at all costs.

In Fear of a Word

Proselytizing received its bad name from unfortunate encounters experienced by Jews during the Diaspora. It is difficult to comprehend that in the last 800 years half of the Jews born into the world have been murdered. Compounding the immensity of the tragedy, and bringing it very close to home, is the fact that over the last 50 years one out of every three Jews has been killed. In addition to such barbaric slaughter, Jewish people live with vivid reminders of being expelled from most European nations at one time or another over the last eight centuries.

Today, in the aftermath of the Holocaust, there are less than 14 million Jewish people in the world. Very few are to be found in Germany, Austria, the Czech Republic, Spain, Portugal, or Poland. The broad perception among Jews, and with documentable justification, is that the "church" and "Christians" contributed immeasurably to ravishing the Jews.

The Dark Ages

Anti-Jewish hatred reached a point during the thousand-year period we know as the Middle Ages that Leon Poliakov in his book *The History of Anti-Semitism* refers to as "the crystallization of anti-Semitism in its classic form." The Dutch humanist Erasmus caught the prevailing mood of the era by commenting, "If it is the part of a good Christian to detest the Jews, then we are all good Christians."

For the Jewish people, the Middle Ages were Dark Ages indeed.

It was a time when such preposterous allegations as the infamous "blood libel" was born. Allegations were spread throughout the Roman Church that Jews were profaning the host—a wafer used in the mass and thought to be transformed into the actual body of Christ. Jews were accused of renewing the agony of Christ by burning, stabbing, and generally tormenting the host. An even more serious crime was alleged in the baseless charge that blood libels were committed by Jews who kidnapped innocent Christian children. These children were said to be ritually murdered. Their blood was then drawn to be used in unleavened bread for Passover.

Expulsions from European cities and even entire countries were common occurrences for Jews. In Spain in 1613, for example, Jews who refused Christian baptism were expelled from the country. Jewish children over seven years of age were taken from their families and brought up as Christians. In 1492 Spain would also hold the distinction of saying to every Jewish family in the nation, "Get out!" That order to exit began the long night of the Inquisition for Jews.

Christian Crusaders, who at the turn of the millennium sent waves of mail-clad warriors to the Middle East to wrest control of Jerusalem from the Muslims, wreaked havoc among Jewish people unfortunate enough to fall in their path. During the Shepherd's Crusade (1320), no less than 140 Jewish communities were destroyed. Needless to say, thousands of Jewish lives were lost.

In 1347, when the Black (bubonic) Plague ravaged Europe, causing one-third of the population to perish, Jews were accused of poisoning the wells. Offered as evidence was the seeming immunity of many Jews to the plague. In actuality, many Jewish people escaped the plague because of their strict sanitary practices. Flames of hatred for the accused soared to the point where emperors guaranteed immunity from prosecution to citizens who took it upon themselves to execute Jews. Europe's cleansing process swept away 350 Jewish communities.

With the Middle Ages came the Jewish ghettos, with yellow patches sewn to Jews' clothing as "badges of shame" and bells fastened to Jewish women's skirts so Christians could be warned that a Jewess was approaching. In Germany, Jews were distinguished by being forced to wear pointed hats, while on the streets of Rome Jewish men walked about in red capes, their women in red aprons.

There was, of course, an alternative: Jews could convert to Christianity. There were notable periods when Jews were put in the unenviable position of being forced to convert or die. In contemporary terminology, Jews of the Middle Ages were placed between the proverbial *rock and a hard place.* For many of them, the choice was to convert to Christianity or forfeit all their property. Of course, if they converted to Christianity, they were disinherited by Judaism. Yet refusal to convert meant not only that they were in jeopardy of losing their property, but that they were faced with the gruesome possibility of keeping an appointment with those who burned people at the stake.

Luther and the Jews

The Protestant Reformation, which held some promise of relief for the Jewish people, had its own dark side. Martin Luther at first believed Jews would receive his message and flock to their Messiah—but they did not. Luther's sympathy turned to scorn, and he scalded recalcitrant Jewry in 1542 with his 200-page book *Against the Jews and Their Lies*. His late-in-life diatribe against Jewry endures as the classic expression of the Dark Ages view of the Jews.

> Know, O adored Christ, and make no mistake, that aside from the Devil, you have no enemy more venomous, more desperate, more bitter, than a true Jew.... Let their synagogues be burned, their books confiscated, that they be forbidden to pray to God in their own way, and that they be made to work with their hands, or, better still, that the princes expel them from their lands, and that authorities—magistrates as well as clergy—unite toward these ends.[1]

Thus out of the shadows of the Dark Ages emerged the familiar caricature of the wandering Jew. Threadbare and disheveled, he has shuffled along the lonely road of exile and social isolation across the face of the centuries, moving inexorably toward the Holocaust. Unfortunately, in many locales, and for reasons we shall discuss later, the legacy endures.

Under the Wings of the Divine Presence

Yet in spite of the shabby practices of some who called themselves "Christian," the entire concept of proselytizing—converting from one belief or faith to another—

19

is as ancient a practice as religion itself, and was without question an integral part of Judaism itself until relatively recent history.

A well-known fact found in the biblical record is that Jews actively encouraged people to convert to the Jewish faith. When Jesus castigated some practices of corrupt members of the Temple leadership in Jerusalem, He spoke of them as people who "compass sea and land to make one proselyte" (Matthew 23:15).

Jesus' words reflect the spirit of the times in which He lived and convey an implication for which both Jews and Christians can be profoundly grateful. In fact, one of the most frequently quoted passages in all the Bible are the words of a proselyte to the Jewish faith. Ruth, the Moabite widow of the Jew Mahlon, refused to forsake her mother-in-law Naomi and return to her own land. "Entreat me not to leave thee," Ruth pleaded, "or to turn away from following after thee; for where thou goest I will go, and where thou lodgest I will lodge; thy people shall be my people, and thy God my God. Where thou diest will I die, and there will I be buried" (Ruth 1:16,17).

Beautiful words indeed. But Ruth's oath of allegiance to a new people, a new God, and a new country goes far beyond a simple Moabite woman's personal determination. Ruth, the Gentile who later married Boaz, became the great-grandmother of the illustrious King David. In the New Testament her name appears again in the genealogy of Jesus of Nazareth. Thus Jews and Christians alike can utter appreciation for properly placed proselytes.

Other references to proselytes' faith can be found in the New Testament book of Acts. On the day of Pentecost, when Jews from the known world were in Jerusalem for the feast, celebrants from "Phrygia and Pamphylia in Egypt, and in the parts of Libya about Cyrene" were joined by "sojourners of Rome, both Jews and proselytes" (Acts 2:10).

Perhaps the reference with the most obvious contemporary connotation is seen in a deacon named Philip, who received instructions to journey south from Samaria toward Gaza. "And he arose and went; and, behold, a man of Ethiopia, a eunuch of great authority under Candace, Queen of the Ethiopians, who had the charge of all her treasure and had come to Jerusalem to worship, was returning, and sitting in his chariot read Isaiah the prophet" (Acts 8:27,28). This ancient forebear of the Ethiopians who have recently immigrated to Israel was numbered among a people who were most assuredly proselytes to Judaism. Therefore modern Israel is indebted to some ancient Jewish herald of the faith who must have been eager to bear the good tidings of his religion to people he felt needed to know the God of Abraham, Isaac, and Jacob.

Thus proselytizing in historic context has been practiced with integrity for millennia. It is only as the practice was sullied by pseudo-Christians or others, through unseemly motives and methods, that making one's faith known to others became an odious enterprise.

Throughout Jewish history the proselyte has been a constant presence. While opinions about just how active Jews should be in seeking converts have ebbed and flowed with the centuries (and along with, I might add, opinions of individual rabbis), the question of how to acquire and deal with proselytes is always close at hand.

A statement from the *Encyclopedia Judaica* asserts that "Most of the rabbis of the Talmud observed the tradition: 'When a proselyte comes to be converted, one receives him with an open hand so as to bring him under the wings of the Divine Presence' " (SER 7; Lev. R. 2:9).

Some rabbis felt so strongly about bringing Gentiles "under the wings of the Divine Presence" that they came to believe that an essence of Israel's dispersion was to win converts. Third-century rabbis Johanan and Eleazar separately articulated the conviction: "The Holy One, Blessed be He, exiled Israel among the nations only in order to increase their numbers with the addition of proselytes" (Pes. 87b). Rabbi Eleazar also said, "Whoever befriends a proselyte is considered as if he created him" (Gen. R. 84:4).

Terminology associated with the conversion of Gentiles to Judaism paralleled, in some respects, the Christian view regarding converts to Christianity. This is seen in the fact that a Gentile convert "is considered a newly born child." Henceforth he was no longer associated with former family ties but became "the son of Abraham."

The revered Jewish sage Maimonides, in comforting a proselyte who was being harassed, wrote, "Toward father and mother we are commanded honor and reverence, toward the prophets to obey them, but toward proselytes we are commanded to have great love in our inmost hearts....God, in His glory, loves proselytes." Those Gentiles who "pursued God...and entered beneath the wings of the Divine Presence...the Lord does not call you fool, but intelligent and understanding, wise and walking correctly, a pupil of Abraham our father."

Today, following decades of a self-defensive attitude toward the whole idea of active proselytizing, some segments of Jewry consider a return to seeking converts a desirable pursuit.

The first incorporated Jewish missionary society in modern times, the United Israel World Union, was founded in New York City in 1944. Another such missionary society, the Jewish Information Society of America, was founded in Chicago in 1962. Reform Judaism in the United States has reportedly promoted the idea that Jews have an obligation to teach their religion to all mankind and to attract like-minded non-Jews into the Jewish community. The Conservative rabbinate, however, does not share this view, although they do accept prospective converts. The Orthodox are extremely reluctant to receive converts, making conversion a very stringent process.

Assimilation: Judaism's Greater Dilemma

Jews in both the United States and Israel are facing very serious questions about their future attitude and practice on the issue of proselytizing. Jewry's primary problem in America is not how many Jewish people are becoming Christians. The main problem currently confronting them is *assimilation*. Every other Jewish person in America is now marrying a Gentile—a fact causing grave concern to the rabbinate. The question is how to bring these people into Judaism and active Jewish community life.

In Israel, the influx of large numbers of Russian Jews who are bringing non-Jewish wives and relatives into the country is raising havoc with traditional practices. A 1970 amendment to the Law of Return included partners, children, and grandchildren of mixed marriages, who were not Jewish according to religious law, as legal citizens of the country. The situation has, in Jewish terms, "made the need for an acceleration of proselytization urgent."

The point to be drawn from all this is that proselytizing is not inherently something to be seen as the foulest of enterprises. Nor is it a practice adopted to maliciously degrade or destroy a race of people. All people who value, especially in an eternal frame of reference, the message committed to them have an obligation to communicate that message to others. The fact that they do it is not the problem. It is *how* they do it, and their attitude toward those who refuse their message, that tends to create lingering hostility.

New Testament Anti-Semitism?

We are often faced with the question of anti-Semitism in the New Testament. We must candidly say that those who have conspired to buffet Jewish people, such as the Ku Klux Klan and Neo-Nazis, often select verses from the New Testament that they feel provide a rationale for their agendas.

Such groups tend to be of the same ilk as certain mainline liberal Protestant theologians, who have indicted Judaism as an unworthy, "bloody" religion because of the conflicts between ancient Israel and its enemies recorded in the Old Testament. Of course, this sort of thinking is as much a breeding ground for anti-Semitism as is inflammatory rhetoric from unsavory fanatics at the other end of the spectrum.

In answer to the question about New Testament anti-Semitism, let us examine two often-cited examples.

But first let's consider an observation by Irvin J. Borowsky, Founder and Chairman of the American Interfaith Institute. Borowsky, who is himself Jewish, makes a telling point.

> Jesus did not fear his fellow Jews. He feared those in authority who were abusing their own people. In fact…some of the words in the New Testament have been used by people in power to arouse mobs to burn synagogues and kill Jews.
>
> The facts are clearly documented. Judea in the first century was a nation occupied by the Roman Empire. And, as in every occupation, a small number of citizens chose to work for those in power. They were supported by the Romans as priests, money changers, and tax collectors. They shared the proceeds that they

extracted from their fellow Jews with the Roman authorities.

It was this small group of Jews that Jesus opposed....Jesus lived and died an observant Jew....He was only critical of those who were exploiting his fellow Jews.[2]

This would certainly shed light on the famous episode of Jesus' exchange with livid money changers and Temple authorities when He turned over their tables and drove their sheep from the stalls in the Court of the Gentiles at Passover. Why He was not immediately apprehended cannot be explained, except in light of what the corrupt Temple authorities had been doing to Jewish worshipers. Their response to His action was to say simply, "What sign showest thou unto us, seeing that thou doest these things?" (John 2:18). Luke implies that they feared the people—faith-inspired worshipers who had had enough of being exploited by their own shepherds (Luke 19:48).

That certain statements by Jesus and other New Testament writers were directed at corrupt elements, and not at Jewry in general, is an extremely important point.

The debilitating accusation that the Jews killed Christ and therefore successive Jewish generations bear personal responsibility for the crucifixion has been the source of untold suffering for innocent Jewish people. Anti-Semites often buttress their call to fight the "Christ killers" by appealing to an incident recorded in the New Testament. When the Temple leadership was accusing Jesus before Pilate—following Pilate's famous washing of his hands and declaring, "I am innocent of the blood of this righteous person"—the people responded this way: "Then answered all the people and said, His blood be on us, and on our children" (Matthew 27:24,25).

Their answer is viewed as reason enough to say, two

millennia later, that Jewish people should bear the stigma of "Christ killer" called down upon them by their forebears.

The New Testament records facts rather than issuing an indictment. Even casual readers can learn, by simply reading the text, that the people were incited by leaders who were zealous to achieve what they had come to accomplish. This is seen in Matthew 27:20: "But the chief priests and elders persuaded the multitude that they should ask for Barabbas and destroy Jesus." We can be sure that these same leaders were exhorting the crowd to call for Jesus' blood to be upon them and their children.

Another verse, never appealed to by anti-Semites, tells an entirely different story about significant numbers of Jewish people in Jesus' day: "And the common people heard him gladly" (Mark 12:37).

The idea that there was a significant amount of corruption among the Temple authorities is well-documented by sources other than the New Testament.

The historian Josephus described as "a great hoarder up of money" one of the relatives of the high priest who garnered profits from money–changing and the sale of sacrificial animals at the Temple. The Talmud makes a figurative lament about such corrupters of the sanctuary by crying out, "Cause the sons of Eli, Hophni and Phinehas to depart hence, for they defiled the Temple" (Keritoth 28a).

In short, we can conclude that, whatever the source of the incitement, no group of leaders can impose a blanket condemnation upon generations yet unborn; to attempt to do so is simply preposterous. It is as unfair to accuse Jewish people of personal participation in the crucifixion as it is to accuse all Christians of condoning the horrors of the Holocaust and to conclude that their efforts to make Christ known to Jews are somehow comparable to Hitler's program of extinction.

I am personally convinced that engaging in vehement

attacks against Jews, and employing the Bible as a reason for doing so, goes far beyond irrational ignorance—it is too pervasive a manifestation. It is at its heart demonic, if for no other reason than that it is so ludicrous an assertion.

A few months ago, after giving a lecture on the Middle East in a Midwestern city, I was approached by a young man who was agitated over some positions I had presented. Following the standard monologue about Jewish untrustworthiness, he summed up by saying that, after all, Jews killed Jesus—in short, they were "Christ killers."

My response, and I don't know exactly why I said it, was, "And what nationality are you?"

"Italian," he immediately replied.

"Italian?" I said. "Has anyone ever called you a 'Christ killer'?"

"Of course not," he fumed.

"Well, using your line of reasoning, you could as quickly be indicted as a 'Christ killer' as you do the Jews."

"I've never heard an Italian called a 'Christ killer,'" he said.

"Nor is it likely you ever will," I countered. "It serves no one's purpose to do so. But the fact is that it was Gentile Roman legionnaires, sent to the Middle East from the place of your forebears by the emperor, who physically impaled Christ on the cross.

"But, while what I have just told you is a historic fact, it gives no one the right, 2000 years later, to call you a 'Christ killer.' You have every right to deeply resent the implication. No more so, however, than the Jewish people you have just accused."

"Ye are of your father the devil, and the lusts of your father ye will do" (John 8:44). While recently viewing a film on hate groups, I heard a burly, white-sheeted Ku Klux Klan leader bawling this quotation to a small cadre of fellow fanatics standing in a circle around a burning, burlap-swathed cross. His message was unembellished: If you're for God, you must be against Jews—the Bible tells us so.

I realize that it will do no good to attempt a contextual, biblical rebuttal to such people. They would believe every Jew was personally fathered by the devil himself regardless of any evidence to the contrary. Like their radical Middle Eastern soul mates, they hate Jews because they hate Jews.

For the benefit of the rest of us, clearly Jesus was speaking to some of the leaders mentioned above, who were in the process of accusing Him of being a demonized Samaritan. His work had nothing to do with the Jewish people in general or their descendants.

The truth is, as we have observed, that people with less-than-honorable intentions are seldom above employing less-than-honorable means to get or do what they want.

Reputable pastors and teachers of the New Testament, however, should make their hearers clearly aware of just who was on the receiving end of such words and the limits of Jesus' intent.

2

Specter of the Holocaust

The aforementioned people, with less-than-honorable intentions, are not a dying breed. As a consequence, the specter of the Holocaust is a constant companion of the Jewish people. Unfortunately, visions of the catastrophic mutilation of Jewry is not a thing that rises out of the mists of antiquity. No indeed. Jews and Gentiles need look back only a half century to see twin monsters that are unsurpassed in all of human history for brutality. Adolf Hitler and the killing machines of his Third Reich systematized genocide to the point that the memories of six million dead Jews have been rolled into one ominously encompassing word—Holocaust.

Today enormous efforts are being launched by revisionists in an attempt to declare the Holocaust a myth, while at the same time raising the memory of Adolf Hitler to some level of historical credibility. Furthermore, there are great misperceptions among many Jewish people about the religious identity of the perpetrators of the slaughter of Jewish people in the World War II era.

This being true, it becomes necessary to provide an extended, but I trust not laborious, examination of the Holocaust question and expose just who Adolf Hitler was and what he and his Reich were all about.

A few years ago I sat at lunch with a young friend in a restaurant in Jerusalem. Yoram, who holds a graduate degree from the Hebrew University in Jewish-Christian Relations, was assisting me with some research in the Zionist Archives. On that particular day our conversation turned to religion and divergent views on some points of theology in Christianity and Judaism. "What," I asked, "is your general view of Christianity?"

"I know a great deal about Christianity," Yoram responded. "But I don't think you'd like to hear my honest opinion. We're friends; let's drop the subject."

"No," I replied, "I'd rather not drop the subject. I really would like to hear your opinion."

"Well," he began, "we are seated here in the city of Jerusalem. When your people [Crusaders] came to this city in 1099 to establish a kingdom for Jesus, they burned Jews alive in their synagogues, massacred others, and sold the rest into slavery.

"During the Black Death in Europe in the 1300s, Jews were accused of poisoning the wells of Christians. This resulted in thousands of Jews being put to death.

"In 1492 the Christian rulers Ferdinand and Isabella ordered every Jew in Spain to get out. The Inquisition was a deadly exercise in expulsion and terror. I can tell you stories of Jews who left their homes with nothing but the clothes on their backs. To survive the cold nights, they were forced to dig pits in manure heaps and bury themselves.

"Polish Cossacks slaughtered at least 100,000 of my people in the Ukraine in 1648. Such pogroms seemed to become almost as common as sunrise for Jews.

"I could go on, but let me finish with this. In your lifetime and mine, from the country that was for centuries the seat of Christian theology—Germany—came the Holocaust, the greatest bloodbath my people have ever known. And after all, Elwood, wasn't Adolf Hitler himself a Christian?"

Was Hitler a Christian?

Adolf Hitler was perceived by my intellectual Jewish friend, and countless others, as a Christian. In Yoram's mind, and for millions of Jewish people, the centuries-old road of "Christian" persecution of their kinsmen was but a tortuous climb toward the pinnacle reached when Hitler proclaimed the infamous "final solution." With the extermination of 6 million Jews within the very bastions of European Christian enlightenment came the all-but-universal "case closed" attitude of Jewry toward their Christian counterparts.

To say that Adolf Hitler hated Jews stands among the classic understatements of human history. His venom toward Jewry and his passion for their extermination are set forth in the self-aggrandizing ramblings of his book, *Mein Kampf* (My Struggle), which would one day become the bible of the Third Reich. The true spirit of the man, his mission, and the book he produced is captured succinctly by Konrad Heiden, who wrote the introduction for the Houghton Mifflin edition. "The book," he said, "may well be called a kind of satanic Bible. To the author...the belief in human equality is a kind of hypnotic spell exercised by world-conquering Judaism with the help of Christian churches." In Hitler's twin indictment of Jews and churches, he exposed the very soul of his mania. The Jew would become his first target of opportunity.

"Was there any form of filth or profligacy, particularly in cultural life, without at least one Jew involved in it?" he wrote.

"If you cut even cautiously into such an abscess, you found, like a maggot in a rotting body, often dazzled by the light—a kike!" (*Mein Kampf*, p. 57).

Anti-Semitism cut so deeply into the fiber of Adolf Hitler's life that he saw himself as the sole avenger of alleged Jewish misdeeds—the Creator's very angel of death.

"Hence today," he raved, "I believe that I am acting in accordance with the will of the Almighty Creator: by defending myself against the Jew, I am fighting for the work of the Lord" (*Mein Kampf*, p. 65).

Before Allied military forces and death entered to cut short his grotesque mission, the blood of 6 million Jews would testify to the Fuehrer's deadly seriousness of purpose. By anyone's standard of analysis, this was not the work of someone who calls himself a man of God, Christian or otherwise.

Indeed, the memory of the Holocaust remains such a painful episode that it is almost impossible for the mind to assimilate the immensity of cruelty and suffering endured by Hitler's victims. Perhaps this is why revisionist historians, who deny that the Holocaust ever happened, are receiving a hearing today for their preposterous and dangerous distortions.

Faded Numbers, Indelible Memories

As long as there remains among us a host of Jewish elders who still bear on their arms the faded blue numbers from the death camps, the world will have a witness. But when they, and those who were eyewitnesses to their agony, are gone, we can anticipate a torrent of denial from anti-Semites and those with no stomach for historic reality.

A few months ago I received a hefty packet of photographs from a World War II veteran who had served in the infantry. The photos were grisly scenes of Jewish bodies stacked in discordant piles. Their vacant stares were indifferent to their nakedness before the young soldiers who had entered the barbed–wire enclosures where Jews had been penned up to die. General Eisenhower had wisely ordered them brought to the death camps to view the carnage that had taken place. "Take a good look at what they have done," the young GIs were told, "and when you go home, don't let us forget what happened here."

The aging veteran was concerned. He had been hearing and reading that it had never happened. The Holocaust was a fiction created by Zionist schemers intent on manipulating international sympathies. "I know it happened," he wrote. "I saw it for myself. But what will happen when we are all gone? Who will answer them?"

He was correct. Consequently, now is the time for Jewish people and Christians who know the facts to set the record straight and produce new volumes of irrefutable facts, figures, and graphic memorials to that which we can ill afford to forget. To do so would most certainly will to the next generation the awful prospect of history repeating itself.

The Will to Kill

In his final days, hunkered down in his bunker with Berlin burning around him, Hitler still ranted against Jewry. So deeply did the dictator despise the children of Abraham that he wrote them into his will. "Above all," he instructed, "I enjoin the leaders of the nation and those under them to uphold racial laws to their full extent and to expose mercilessly the universal poisoner of all peoples, international Jewry." So absolute was his demented contempt for the

Jewish people that he believed, should Jews gain control of the political systems of the world, that the planet would be denuded of human beings. "Should the Jew," Hitler said, "triumph over the people of this world, his crown will be the funeral wreath of mankind, and the planet will once again follow its orbit through the ether, without any human life on its surface, as it did millions of years ago."

Personal hatred for a race of people, as lamentable as it may be, is one thing. It is quite another to systematize such vehemence as a political weapon that feeds ingrained prejudices while diverting prying eyes from the true objectives of the regime. The sound and fury of the onslaught of the Nazi "scapegoat the Jew" campaign at the same time caused a credulous nation to become deaf and blind to the plight of European Jewry. "There must," the future Fuehrer raved in a Munich beer hall cellar in 1920, "be a new slogan, one not restricted to Germany alone—Anti-Semites of the world, unite! People of Europe, free yourselves." He also called for what he coined a "thorough solution...the removal of the Jews from the midst of our people." As we ponder how such a program of political genocide could be launched without the general population knowing what was happening, the answer cannot be that the country did not understand what Hitler intended to do. William H. Shirer in his book *The Rise and Fall of the Third Reich* makes the point: "Whatever accusations can be made against Adolf Hitler, no one can accuse him of not putting down in writing exactly the kind of Germany he intended to make if he ever came to power and the kind of world he meant to create by armed German conquest."

How then could people who knew his intentions and saw what Hitler was doing tolerate the brutality taking place before their eyes?

In a postscript to his book *Der Führer*, Konrad Heiden

offers a perceptive explanation.

> Hitler was able to enslave his own people because he seemed to give them something that even the traditional religions could no longer provide: the belief in a meaning to existence beyond the narrowest self-interest. The real degradation began when people realized that they were in league with the Devil, but felt that even the Devil was preferable to the emptiness of an existence which lacked larger significance.[3]

The German Church

Although he was born a Roman Catholic, the state which the Fuehrer meant to create was to be anything but Christian. He took a rather dim view of the potential worth of Protestants as allies in matters nearest his heart—namely, de-Judaizing the planet. While commending Protestantism's resolve to advance Germanism in matters of personal purity, Hitler questioned their commitment to opposing Jews.

> ...[Protestantism] combats with the greatest hostility any attempt to rescue the nation from the embrace of its most mortal enemy, since its attitude toward the Jews just happens to be more or less dogmatic. Yet here we are facing the question without whose solution all other attempts at a German reawakening or resurrection are and remain absolutely senseless and impossible.[4]

Hitler proposed that the very Jews he so despised had devised strategies that pitted Protestants and Catholics against one another. "With miraculous speed he [the Jew] threw the torch of discord into the folkish [Ayran] movement and sowed dissension. In any case the Jew reached his desired goal: Catholics and Protestants wage a merry war with one another, and the mortal enemy of Aryan humanity and all Christendom laughs up his sleeve." So while Jews systematically practice "this contamination of our blood...the two denominations do not fight today against the destroyer of this man, but strive mutually to annihilate one another. The folkish-minded man, in particular, has the sacred duty, each in his own denomination, of making people stop just talking superficially of God's will, and actually fulfill God's will, and not let God's word be desecrated" (*Mein Kampf*, pp. 560, 562).

What Hitler was calling Catholics and Protestants to do "in fulfilling God's will" distilled into nothing less than joining him in the annihilation of Jewry.

Despite all his talk about discord sown by Jews and indecision among Protestants, he would later discover, when National Socialism became the political reality in Germany, that many among the clergy—Protestant and Catholic—would follow the swastika along with his goose-stepping minions.

What Hitler and his Nazi followers were about to introduce into German life was a new religion, a religion that, by any term chosen—it would be called the German Church—was no more than a cult of the Fuehrer. As history bears witness, whenever such a religion of politics, with an antichristlike figure at its head, comes to the scene, Jews are prime targets against whom to vent imperial wrath and popular frustrations. Self-created saviors must always have both a visible enemy against whom to pit themselves as deliverers and followers who are determined champions of his cause. More often than not, it seems, Jewry has been at hand to play the role of scapegoat. Hitler's version played like this.

The Jew's domination of the state seems so assured that now not only can he call himself a Jew again but he ruthlessly admits his ultimate national and political designs. A section of his race openly owns itself to be a foreign people, yet even here they lie. For while the Zionists try to make the rest of the world believe that the national consciousness of the Jew finds satisfaction in the creation of a Palestinian state, the Jews again slyly dupe the dumb *Goyim* [Gentiles]. It doesn't even enter their heads to build up a Jewish state in Palestine for the purpose of living there; all they want is a central organization for their international world swindle, endowed with its own sovereign rights and removed from the intervention of other states: a haven for convicted scoundrels and a university for budding crooks.[5]

Protocols of the Learned Elders

A primer that Hitler used for "exposing the Jewish international conspiracy" was a pamphlet titled *The Protocols of the Learned Elders of Zion.* He viewed these elders as the authentic revelation of the international Jewish conspiracy. "To what extent," he wrote, "the whole existence of this people [Jews] is based on a continuous lie is shown incomparably by the *Protocols of the Wise Men of Zion*" (*Mein Kampf,* p. 307).

I mention the *Protocols* here because, in addition to being used by Hitler as a rationale to exterminate Jews, it is still today a primary reference source for the most vehement anti-Semites on earth. In fact, I have in hand a recent edition of the book produced in Canada for distribution in North America.

The *Protocols* are being quoted and distributed by such anti-Semitic groups as the neo-Nazis, the Ku Klux Klan, Aryan Nations, Christian Identity, Muslims, and a host of marginal fellow travelers, many of whom call themselves Christians. The level of potential volatility disseminated through the pamphlet can be illustrated in what Israel is currently experiencing.

It is well-known that the radical Muslim extremist groups Hamas, Islamic Jihad, and assorted others used the *Protocols* as justification for killing Jews—even to the point of dispatching suicide bombers to achieve their purpose. In an extensive interview with members of Islamic Jihad at their headquarters in Gaza, journalist Tim Timmerman heard repeated references to the *Protocols*. The *Protocols*, he was informed, proved that the Zionists were plotting to rule the world and destroy Muslims. Six days later Hishman Ismail Hamed, a 21-year-old university student who had attended the meeting and spoken with Timmerman, rode his bomb-laden bicycle into an Israeli Army checkpoint in Gaza, killing himself and three Israeli soldiers.

The infamous document, produced by the czarist intelligence service in Russia more than 90 years ago, has been repeatedly exposed as a concocted forgery produced to legitimatize persecution of Jews. The *Protocols* are purported to be a report of 24 meetings held in Basel, Switzerland, in 1897, at the time of the First Zionist Congress. Plans were said to have been developed there in which Jews would disrupt the entire Christian civilization and, on the ruins of Christendom, erect a world state ruled over by Jews. Various devices are described that the Jews planned to use, among them the use of liquor to befuddle the European leaders' opinions, the corruption of European womanhood, stirring up economic distress, and planning to blow up a number of European capitals.

In a report prepared for the Committee on the Judiciary of the United States Senate in 1964, the *Protocols* were denounced as yet another of the "fabricated 'historic documents' which have been foisted on an unsuspecting public for some malign purpose." The committee concluded that "it is impossible for a fair-minded person of any common sense not to see that the *Protocols* are the fictional product of a warped mind."

Sad to say, such preposterous products of warped minds can become instruments of inestimable destruction—as the *Protocols* continue to be today.

A Christian Atrocity?

Considering all the facts mentioned so far in this chapter, how did the perception of the Holocaust as a "Christian" atrocity occur? For one thing, Hitler was, as has been pointed out, a nominal Catholic. In the days preceding World War II, the Catholic Church still stigmatized Jews as "Christ killers." Among Protestants, the legacy of Martin Luther's diatribes against the Jewish people was alive and well. Thus Hitler was able to successfully exploit a strain of anti-Semitic tendencies that were fixed in the minds of various segments of the Catholic and Protestant communities in Germany.

An even more compelling factor involved the withering assaults on the Bible and biblically orthodox Christianity being delivered by liberal theologians and their secular-humanist bedfellows. Yes, Germany had once been a center of orthodox biblical theology, but the ravages of liberalism had taken their toll and sapped the spiritual vitality from hosts of Germans. With the biblical dynamic denied them, it is little wonder that many nominally religious Germans turned to the state and sat mesmerized among the masses who listened to a man who knew what he believed.

This is a point that is sometimes lost to a generation half a century removed from the scene. We see the grim photos and vicious documents and wonder why so many Germans fell in line behind a madman. One reason among many was his ability to articulate in a compelling fashion what he deeply believed. Hitler was able to make the absurd sound sublime. In the aftermath of World War I and the national humiliation that overcame the proud German people, they needed a hero. They found their man in Adolf Hitler, and when he took the rostrum to strut and rant, the great stadiums of the Fatherland shook with "Sieg Heil!"

An ocean away, I remember as a boy hearing those speeches as they came over the radio. I could not understand his German, but I was transfixed by Hitler's voice with its consuming transmission of confidence and authority.

Swept up in the pomp and pageantry of the Third Reich, many professing Christians were obviously becoming less than incensed at events taking place around them.

Then, too, the relentless Nazi anti-Jewish propaganda, coupled with the early political and military triumphs of the regime, conditioned much of the populace to the point that what was happening to their Jewish neighbors did not seem to be a major concern to them. Furthermore, the fact that the Vatican and major Protestant denominations either initially cooperated or were neutralized until it was much too late to make a difference will forever stand in stark contradiction to everything Christ and His church rightly represent. Nonetheless, the perception that somehow Christians were coconspirators endures, and it is an issue that must be addressed.

It is imperative to note that the relatively few people (some will be specifically mentioned later) who stood as Christians against Hitler and his madness were almost invariably those who had not given up their commitment to the Word of God. Rather, they appealed to Scripture for their mandate to stand with the Jewish people and against Nazism.

Lords of the Earth

The Third Reich's brand of religion was designed to destroy and then replace what we might term *conventional Christianity*. This was amply illustrated in Hitler's relationship with a man named Houston Stewart Chamberlain, a nephew of England's Sir Neville Chamberlain. It was commonly said that H. S. Chamberlain was the spiritual founder of the Third Reich. He saw Germans as the master race and their leader as a man sent from God to lead the German people out of the wilderness. Chamberlain's theological views were, to say the least, strange. "Whoever claimed," he said, "that Jesus was a Jew was either being stupid or telling a lie.... Jesus was not a Jew." When asked who Jesus was, He replied, "Probably an Aryan! If not entirely by blood, then unmistakably by reason of his moral and religious teaching." Chamberlain went so far as to propose that the important personalities in Jewish history, such as David and the prophets, were of Germanic descent.

The Germanic obsession with racial superiority—breeding and populating the planet with racially pure "Lords of the Earth"—called for the birth of a new religion. Adolf Hitler, who frequently used the term "Lords of the Earth," saw himself as the perfect Caesar-god.

By the late 1930s it was clear that the Nazis intended to destroy Christianity in Germany. Martin Bormann and Heinrich Himmler, encouraged by Hitler, promoted a return to the old paganism of the early tribal Germanic gods and a brand of neopaganism created by Nazi fanatics. In 1941 Bormann stated publicly that "National Socialism and Christianity are irreconcilable."

Bormann and his goose-stepping peers were not alone in their extremism. Dr. Reinhardt Krause, the Berlin district leader of the "German Christians," proposed the abandonment of the Old Testament. He further championed a revision of the New Testament in which the teachings of Jesus would be made to correspond "entirely with the demands of National Socialism." Hitler's "German Church" heard resolutions calling for "One People, One Reich, One Faith." Compliant pastors were required to take an oath of allegiance to the Fuehrer and, among other things, exclude converted Jews from their churches.

Dr. Hans Kerrl, a Nazi lawyer, was appointed Minister of Church Affairs in 1935. Kerrl's task was to reconcile Protestants with the master program for the German Church. His view of Christianity provides a window to the very soul of National Socialism.

> The [Nazi] party stands on the basis of positive Christianity, and positive Christianity *is* National Socialism....National Socialism is the doing of God's will....God's will reveals itself in German blood....Faith in Christ as the Son of God. That makes me laugh....No, Christianity is not dependent on the Apostles' Creed....True Christianity is represented by the party, and the German people are now called by the party and especially by the Fuehrer to a real Christianity....the Fuehrer is the herald of a new revelation.[6]

Portions of Hitler's "new revelation" for Germany were set forth in a 30-point program drawn up for the National Reich Church. Two of the program's points get to the heart of the issues between the Nazi regime and true Christianity. "The National Church demands immediate cessation of the publishing and dissemination of the Bible in Germany" (13). "On the altars there must be nothing but *Mein Kampf* (to the German nation and therefore to God the most sacred book) and to the left of the altar a sword" (19).

To Hitler and his diabolical cronies, the National Reich Church was the perfected Religion of Politics that was destined to serve the "Lords of the Earth" throughout the glorious millennium envisioned for the Third Reich.

The Evangelical Thorn in the Nazi Side

From the beginning, however, there were those Christians—a minority, to be sure—who said no to religious hand-holding with swastika-wielding emissaries of the devil. With names like the Confessional Church, the Pastor's Emergency League, and the Evangelical Church of Germany, some stood against the new wave of nationally enshrined paganism.

Such groups resolutely reaffirmed their belief in the Word of God as their only rule of faith and practice.

As early as January 1933 a group of pastors met and formulated a declaration which boldly said that the Church was called into existence by God, that in it Christ is the living power, that the state is ordained by God to curb man's sinful passions, that no specific form of the state is Christian, that Christians must obey God rather than men, that when the state seeks to dominate the consciences of men it has become anti-Christian, that when political parties assume the form of religion, they do violence to the state, and that

> Christians must resist both the deification of
> the state and any party which seeks absolute
> control over the individual.[7]

This same source points out that the Pastor's
Emergency League, made up largely of younger men,
responded forcefully to what they regarded as the heathen
theology of the German Church. "We refuse," they
affirmed, "to earn the reproach of being dumb dogs. We
owe it to our congregations and to the Church to resist the
falsification of the Gospel. We emphatically recognize the
Holy Scripture of the Old and New Testaments as the
unique test of our faith and life" (p. 26). Such commitment to biblical principles spawned acts of courageous
opposition to the persecution of the Jewish people and
other atrocities, such as state-induced euthanasia.

Hitler's reaction to upstart evangelicals who refused to
bow the knee to their new Caesar was emphatic. The
Fuehrer insisted that if the Nazi-controlled German
Church could not bring evangelical churches into line
with the designs of the new religion, the government itself
would be obligated to take over direction of the churches.

The dictator's idea of *directing* dissident churches was
typically Nazi. By the end of 1935, 700 Confessional
Church pastors were arrested by the Gestapo. Hundreds
more were forced to join them in the concentration camps
in 1936. In 1937, 807 more pastors and leading laymen
were picked up as subversives. Before it was over, thousands of evangelicals attested to the quality of their faith
by choosing death over capitulation or life behind the wire
of the Nazi concentration camps. These people—mostly
unknown and unheralded—march in the ranks of
Righteous Gentiles who could not endure forsaking their
Savior or His Jewish brethren.

Assessing the Insanity

Any attempt to assemble a rational analysis of the Holocaust leaves the mind limp and floating in a sea of frustration. How could it have happened? Why did so many die? Why did so many do so little to stop the slaughter? These questions will, I am convinced, find no substantive answers this side of eternity. But there are some observations we can safely state, and through them see the form of a much larger conflict.

- The Holocaust years proved once again that evil people with designs can capture the minds, bodies, and souls of people all too ready to be duped.
- We stand witness to the fact that the world, for all its protestations of benevolence and concern for the helpless, can go deaf and blind if the helpless are not categorized among the favored few.
- Given a diabolical will and an industrial nation's resources, man can kill in incredible numbers. Treblinka, a death camp in Poland, illustrates this fact. In its 14 months of operation, which began in July 1942, between 750,000 and 870,000 Jews were murdered by a staff of 150 people. There were fewer than a hundred known survivors of Treblinka.
- In the midst of the cruelty, we see monumental acts of personal and national courage. It was demonstrated by those who, like the Nazi industrialist Oskar Schindler, risked everything to save as many Jews as they could. We saw it again on the drawn faces of young GIs, who had crossed an ocean to slog through the carnage of war and rescue people whose names they would never know.
- Perhaps the most gripping human factor was the interminable will of the Jewish people to survive. That demonized men would kill as Hitler and his lackeys

did is mind-numbing enough. But in a very real sense the big story of the Holocaust, beyond the tragedy of the dead, was the survival of the nation of Israel. Although some Jewish survivors still wear on their arms the faded blue numbers of the death camps, they are more than mere survivors. They have seen another generation born and the Zionist dream of a homeland in Palestine become a reality. Hitler, who wished neither the survival of the Jew nor the revival of Jewry's land, was wrong. Adolf Hitler, after all, did not win!

All of this brings us to one final crucial observation: Those who set their face against God's Chosen People will never win the day. Anti-Semitism represents a struggle that surpasses mere human boundaries. As an evangelical committed to the authority of the Word of God, I share the conviction that God has designed a marvelous future for the heirs of Abraham. No satanically driven strategy will stop the nation short of achieving all that the Lord has promised. Although we will examine this subject more fully in a later chapter, suffice it to say here that the preservation of the Jew is a center pole in God's perfect plan for the future.

3

A Walk with the Righteous Gentiles

There is a place in Jerusalem called Yad Vashem, the national Jewish memorial to the Holocaust. It is a place where the world that once was and the world that can happen again are brought into sharp focus.

I stepped into that "world that once was" a few years ago.

In a small apartment in Jerusalem, near Talpiot—where Jews were first settled after the War of Independence—I sat watching a man pace from one side of the room to the other. His gait was rapid; it was as though he were being driven by some force within him to get somewhere in a hurry. Before our visit was over, I found just the opposite to be true. The man was attempting to escape from memories deep inside that refused to let him go.

I was doing research for a book and wanted to interview Holocaust survivors. A friend who was assisting me made arrangements for me to visit a number of his friends who had lived through Hitler's horror. As we approached the apartment door of a man named David, I was cautioned.

"Don't expect this man to say very much. I will tell you his story later."

Our host was a survivor of Auschwitz. David and his small family had been taken into the camp together. He was a skilled woodworker and his wife was a good homemaker and the mother of their treasured infant daughter. His life stopped at Auschwitz, even though he would one day walk out of the place. His body had barely survived; his mind had not. And so there he was 40 years later, smoking incessantly as he paced back and forth across the apartment.

"I come to see him often," my friend said, "and he's always this way.

"His is a bad case, but I can take you to many more who, in one way or another, are like David."

As we left the apartment, I heard his story.

David had committed some small transgression in the camp for which his keepers decided he should be punished. His punishment? To be buried up to his neck in dirt outside the prisoners' barracks. As the guards passed where he was entrapped, some of them kicked his head like a soccer ball.

And then it happened.

David looked up to see his wife, with their daughter in her arms, standing before him. He was puzzled as to why they would bring her there. Perhaps it was to have what they regarded to be fun as they watched her reaction to his situation. Without warning a guard leveled his rifle and shot David's wife through the head. After she fell to the ground, another guard picked up the child, threw her high into the air, and caught her on his bayonet.

Because of his skills as a cabinetmaker, they dug David up, and he survived. But as I saw, his mind would never leave that hole in the ground and the awful spectacle he was forced to witness.

David's is but one story in the sea of 6 million people who perished in the Holocaust. As much as is humanly possible, the Jewish people are determined that the world must never forget, because Jews believe—and a growing number of perceptive Gentiles as well, especially evangelical Christians—that it can happen again.

Revisionists from organizations with reputable-sounding names like The Institute for Historical Review say the Holocaust never happened. These revisionists are pseudo-historians who write fiction, then associate their stories with historical names, dates, and places. These fanciful fabrications are then pawned off on historically illiterate people as fact. Among the most blatant of these fabrications assailing us today purports that the Holocaust never occurred. It is a staple with a variety of anti-Semites whose major occupation in life is, as was Adolf Hitler's, to link the Jewish people to every vice or vicious enterprise in existence.

Yad Vashem sets the record straight.

There, among the carob trees, cypress, and Jerusalem pine, the Jewish people have created a memorial. It is to Jerusalem and this generation what Masada causes people to remember of events that took place atop that sterile plateau two millennia ago. It was at Masada—after the Romans had reduced Jerusalem to rubble and besieged some 360 Jewish holdouts who took refuge in what had been a Herodian fortress—that a fateful decision was made. The beleaguered Jews chose death over humiliation, rape, and enslavement.

It is to Masada that Jews from all over the world go to remember. Gentiles who visit the place are educated.

There they become eyewitnesses to just how far tyrants will go to exterminate people who refuse to bend the knee before them. From Masada's heights, the modern State of Israel makes its declaration to the world: It will never be repeated—Masada, never again!

The Masada Epic

The Masada epic illuminates the larger issues of anti-Semitism and, we must believe, the struggle that transcends our horizons. With the biblical and historical information available to us, there must be a contest moving toward a clarifying consummation.

Allow me to explain.

In 66 A.D. the Romans, who were then masters in Palestine, made a serious mistake. Gessius Florus, procurator of Judea, chose a course of cruel repression of the Jews, who were already rebelling against unbearable Roman repression. The last straw fell when his troops raided the Temple in Jerusalem, removed funds from the sanctuary, and massacred many inhabitants of the city.

This precipitated an all-out rebellion that brought the full weight of the Roman military colossus rumbling into Israel. Vespasian, the finest human weapon in the arsenal and the future emperor, led crack legionnaires against the Jewish rebels. By August of 70 A.D. the hammer fell on the beleaguered Jews, and the struggle for freedom—hopeless from the start—was concluded.

Roman legions breached the walls of Jerusalem and slowly cut their way to the heart of the city. When they reached the Temple site, which was actually a minifortress itself, soldiers broke through and put the sanctuary to the torch. Their infamous act reverberated far beyond the limits of Jerusalem or, for that matter, Israel. With the destruction of the Temple in Jerusalem, the very heart of Judaism was torn from its breast.

As triumphant legionnaires were looting the smolder-
ing ashes of what remained of the Temple, Jewish
escapees were winding their way toward the Dead Sea
and Masada, seeking refuge from the wrath of Rome.
What then transpired is, from a strictly human perspective, perplexing.

Fewer than 400 people were successful in making the
journey to the deserted, plateaued fortress from which
they could look down at the sterile sea 1300 feet below.
There they felt that, well–supplied with food, they would
be safe from the Romans. But it was not to be. Rome did
not allow their presence to go unnoticed, for the emperor
was upset.

His response was to dispatch the storied Tenth Roman
Legion to the foreboding desert wilderness to bring down
the ragamuffin band of Jews. His intent was to parade the
remnants of the rebels through the streets of the imperial
city as tokens of Roman superiority. It would take Rome's
finest three full years to get the job done.

In the process they placed military encampments
around the base of Masada and built a wall that cut it off
completely from the surrounding area. The object was to
make it impossible for even one Jew to escape the clutches
of Rome. Relics of the camps and wall can be seen 2000
years later. However, the greatest monument to Roman
ingenuity and dogged determination is seen in the
remains of the siege ramp the Romans constructed. It
rises from the level of the Dead Sea to the crest of the
plateau. The ramp had sufficient width to accommodate
the massive catapults from which the legionnaires would
batter the outer walls of the fortress. With their weapons
of destruction in place, the issue was soon settled. Rome
had won the day, and Masada was history.

But the question is, Why?

Why would Caesar—who sat as a god on a throne in

control of a massive empire—care about a few Jews perched atop a barren rock in a far-off wilderness? They posed no military threat to him or his legions in Judea. The issue had been settled, the rebellion quelled. His legionnaires had had their triumphal procession through the streets of Rome bearing artifacts from the Temple in Jerusalem. Those emblems of Jewry and their God would be placed in a pagan temple in the imperial city. Word was on the street throughout the empire: The gods of Rome had bested the God of Israel; Jewry's forces had been smashed. It was all there for the world to see and talk about. Rome ruled supreme.

There was, however, one matter unresolved. A few Jews were not on their knees in subservience to the empire and its Caesar. Numbers were therefore inconsequential. There were still Jews in rebellion, and until that matter was disposed of, Rome could never feel secure.

Call it imperial paranoia, if you will. Most certainly, Roman conduct certified that assertion. Looking back across the centuries and the sordid record of persistent anti-Semitism, it is difficult to escape the thought that something more sinister was afoot. Masada seems to depict a larger evil, for in a symbolic sense from that place a march began that would stain the centuries with the blood of Jews. Nearly 2000 years later it causes us to remember Masada and another more fearsome Holocaust at this place called Yad Vashem.

These events and subsequent history verify a persistent demonic obsession to annihilate Jewry on the one hand, and on the other hand the divine determination to preserve the Chosen People and to consummate Israel's ultimate destiny. In simple terms, we are involved in a Satan-God conflict. Masada and Yad Vashem give eloquent evidence to the reality of this battle.

Halls of Remembrance

Yad Vashem stands as a solemn sanctuary of remembrance. There people are reminded that after nearly 2000 years, tyrants not far removed from the seat of ancient Roman imperialism attempted a replay of Masada. Yet they too failed to wipe out the nation of Israel. The residue of their failure provides grim reminders of those who suffered indescribable agony on their way to the chambers of death and that what happened to them can happen again.

Of all the halls of remembrance housed at Yad Vashem, one hall captures the essence of the horrors of the Holocaust in a way different from the others. At the memorial for the children, there are no incriminating documents and only a few photographs to tell their story.

Upon entering, the visitor sees a small gallery of faces—faces of children. Passing them, and moving into the main section of the memorial, you find yourself in a darkened room. It is totally devoid of light except for a few candles burning in the center of the room. The candles reflect tiny bursts of light, which are sent back to the visitor from thousands of pieces of glass extending from floor to ceiling. It is as though you are standing outside on a clear night, looking into a sky filled with stars, each sending back flashes of brilliance from light–years away. For a moment you are apt to be puzzled, as I was. What does this mean? Then it strikes you: Over a muted speaker names are being read, the names of the children, their ages at the time of death, and their countries of origin—1 1/2 million in all. There are no stories of survival in this hall, only the names of victims—children, much like our own. But there is a gulf between them and ours: They were Jewish boys and girls who happened to be in the wrong place at the wrong time.

They were exterminated just because they were Jews.

Unfading Memories

I have stood inside the memorial to the children at Yad Vashem with survivors of the Holocaust. They are the people of the numbers—those marked by purple numerical tattoos, tattoos that set them apart from everyone else alive on earth today. Their numbers are faded now, having turned from purple to a hazy blue. The memories, however, are as fresh as yesterday, and I'm sure every survivor wishes they would, like the numbers, fade.

I was there one day with a friend, a Holocaust survivor from Poland. We didn't say much, since conversation seemed totally inappropriate. I couldn't help wondering what was going through his mind. We were looking at pictures of the faces of children in the foyer. One was frail and blond, appearing to me to look much like my friend would have as a child. *What does he think*, I thought, *when he looks at this boy who would have been around his age at the time of the war?*

As a child, my friend had played happily in the streets of Warsaw. His was a happy family—mom and dad, two sturdy brothers, and a sister. They were all gone now. Adolf Hitler and his Holocaust had seen to that. His two brothers had been hauled away to be worked to death at a camp in Germany. He, at ten years of age, was placed in an orphanage by his mother with the warning never to tell anyone there that he was a Jew.

Their home was confiscated by the Nazis and occupied by people of their choosing. His mother, father, and sister had two more stops to make on the way to annihilation. One was the Warsaw Ghetto. The other, a model of efficiency among Hitler's string of death factories, was Treblinka.

He once told me how he and other children would go into the ghetto searching for relatives. They would enter through the slimy, rodent-infested sewers to avoid being apprehended by guards.

More than a half-million Jews had been stuffed into the Warsaw Ghetto, making the chances of finding relatives slim indeed. The people lived everywhere—in old school buildings, in deserted places of business, and in the streets. Masses of people were living in the streets.

Huddled close to the buildings were the elderly and the very young. Their frail bodies were obviously inching their way toward death. Some seemed to wait quietly, while others lifted feeble hands and uttered pitiful entreaties for help. Now and then, he said, he could hear mumbled prayers for the Messiah to come suddenly and bring deliverance.

Death and disease seemed to stalk everyone in the place. Many people with vacant stares, psychologically scarred beyond the point of return, walked numbly about. Incomprehensible sights and terrible smells cascaded in and out of their minds as they hurried up and down the streets.

A grating clatter of steel on pavement drew his attention to the whole horrible essence of the ghetto. It met him head-on in the middle of the street. He looked up to see a pushcart manned by two men with handkerchiefs over their faces. Human remains were piled on the cart like cordwood. Arms and legs protruded in grotesque gestures amid expressionless faces that stared openmouthed at the sky.

Perhaps his parents and sister had already taken their final ride with the men of the death crew. Did they die there in the Warsaw Ghetto? Or did they choke out their last breaths standing naked in a stifling gas chamber at Treblinka? He would never know. Nor would any of his fellow seekers of living loved ones on the streets of the ghetto.

Perhaps foremost above every squalid sight to catch his eye in the ghetto was his memory of the children. They were so unlike the happy, squealing horde of playmates he had scuffled with when he had a family, a home, a yard, and streets to run. Children of the ghetto were emaciated and bedraggled; their faces wore veils of anguish; their voices carried tired, desperate entreaties: "I am hungry. Please, please, give me bread."

We were looking into some of those faces, my friend and I, as we stood in the foyer of the children's memorial at Yad Vashem. Was he seeing them as they were—listening to their pathetic cries for bread, remembering the stench, hearing the clatter of the death crew's cart? I'm sure he was.

Whenever I walk the grounds and through the memorials at Yad Vashem and meet elderly Jews sobbing uncontrollably, with faces buried in their hands, I am reminded again that the numbers may have faded, but the memories have not.

When the World
Went Blind and Deaf

In conversations with the grieving and often embittered Holocaust survivors, the question raised many times is: "Why didn't someone help us?" It is a haunting question.

Listening to testimony given in the immediate aftermath of the war, we are struck by the almost universal profession of ignorance of what was happening down the street: Jewish families being yanked from their homes, the stench of decaying bodies and smell of burning flesh, trainloads of Jews with their yellow star of David badges lined up on rail platforms in towns and cities, boxcars loaded with those same Jews rumbling through villages on their way to the death camps. Then there were those volleys of shots into the backs of Jewish heads as they stood before open burial pits. And what of general advertising for Jews, as was done in Poland? Delivering one Jew, Poles were told, was worth a bottle of vodka. It was literally a-Jew-for-a-bottle campaign.

And then there were all those missing persons.

Numbers can't communicate adequately the whole story, but they do give irrefutable proof that demands explanation.

Polish-Soviet Area	4,575,000
Germany	125,000
Austria	65,000
Czechoslovakia	277,000
Hungary, including northern Transylvania	402,000
France	82,000
Belgium	24,000
Luxembourg	700
Italy	7,500
The Netherlands	106,000
Norway	760
Romania	40,000
Yugoslavia	60,000
Greece	65,000
Total Jews Liquidated	5,829,960

Did the non-Jews know? Yes. Did they care? The answer is self-evident.

Proof that the great international powers and local populace were aware of what was taking place is found in the rescue efforts mounted by those who had not gone blind and deaf to the plight of the Jews.

If no one knew that Jews were being slaughtered, how could people in many countries have known that they needed to be rescued?

The Street of the Righteous Gentiles at Yad Vashem testifies to both culpability and courage. The fact that rescuers are recognized speaks eloquently of their courage. That such recognition is given speaks to the guilt of those who killed and those who did not care.

The Street of the Righteous Gentiles

Leaving the central area of the memorials, you find yourself walking along a tree-lined street, one with benches carefully placed where visitors can sit to reflect and regain their composure before leaving. In arranging the memorial in this way, the Jewish people have done something quite remarkable. Before these trees are plaques bearing the names and countries of courageous Gentiles and Christians who helped Jewish people escape from the Nazis. It has been named The Street of Righteous Gentiles.

It is exceedingly appropriate, I believe, that as one exits this place, he does so amid living memorials to mercy and the best that human beings can become this side of eternity. This is entirely appropriate after viewing the grim scenes depicting emaciated bodies in dirty, striped uniforms, appearing more like skeletons than living beings. It is entirely appropriate after seeing the barbed wire enclosures and electrified fences with grotesquely configured bodies flung against them in desperate attempts to terminate the unbearable.

Beyond the ovens, the leering faces of the tormentors of dying Jews who were obviously enjoying their dastardly work, the piles of eyeglasses and mounds of shoes stripped from victims, the displays of soap made from Jewish bodies, and all the unspeakable paraphernalia from the gray killing mills—beyond all of this is fresh air and lush green trees, through them a quiet walkway, and at the base of each tree a small plaque.

What those plaques testify to sweeps past every Jewish

fear and every Gentile atrocity. They say: *Not everyone was blind and deaf to the plight of Jewry. There were Christians of another kind than some you've known and tend to remember most vividly. There were those ready and willing to put their lives on the line to save Jewish people.*

In this there is hope and some measure of assurance for the future. None of us knows exactly what is in store in the short term. Jews can be assured, however, that through whatever comes, there will be some—a remnant—who will not forget or turn from the words of Jesus:

"Greater love hath no man than this, that a man lay down his life for his friends" (John 15:13).

For scores of people whose names grace the plaques along The Street of the Righteous Gentiles, this explains why they did what they did.

Oskar Schindler

The plaque most frequently sought out by those familiar with Steven Spielberg's riveting film *Schindler's List* is that of Oskar Schindler. Although Schindler was not someone we would call a classic evangelical, he developed a compassion toward suffering Jewish people that caused him to risk everything. He spent his fortune literally buying Jews—over a thousand of them—from the Nazis. They worked in his factories and lived to tell their stories after the war.

A former diplomat at the Israel Embassy in Washington, now an ambassador, tells of his father and uncle who were saved by Schindler. At lunch one day in Washington, he told me about his first meeting with the man revered by those he saved.

"I was about ten years old," he said. "My father took me into the room and introduced me to Schindler.

"He did something I will never forget. He placed his hand on my head, looked into my face, and said, 'I could have saved more of them.' "

Corrie and Nina

For evangelicals, a highly familiar name gracing one plaque is that of Holland's Corrie ten Boom. Corrie's famous book *The Hiding Place* chronicles how her father's watchmaker's shop and their home were turned into a haven and way station for Jewish people who were being sought by the Nazis. The ten Booms were among the valiant hosts who literally put their lives on the line to aid distressed Jews, in the hope that they would survive Hitler's onslaught. And many Jewish people they helped did survive. The ten Booms, however, were not so fortunate. Corrie's octogenarian father and her sister Betsie died after their rescue operation was discovered by the Germans. Her father died in custody while still in Holland. Betsie crawled to a slow death in a work camp in Germany.

While writing this book I talked to a Jewess, Nina Katz—herself a Holocaust survivor—about her memories of Corrie ten Boom. Nina was incarcerated by the Germans when but 12 years of age. Before she reached her eighteenth birthday, she had done forced labor at work camps in Poland, Germany, and Czeckoslovakia. Freed by the Russian Army on May 7, 1945, a day before the war ended, Nina came to the United States. Here she has twice served as President of Hadassah and is one of the nation's most prominent speakers at functions memorializing the Holocaust.

Nina, who met Corrie ten Boom many years after the war, immediately found a "soul sister" who had known the agonies of suffering at the hands of the Nazis. "To me," Nina remembers, "she was like a modern-day prophet. Corrie was deeply spiritual. We talked and talked, and, yes, we wept together as we remembered those dark days."

"But, you know, Corrie," Nina told her, "we Jews, because of who we were, had no choice. You and your family did. You knew that if you were caught hiding Jews, it would cost you your life. Still you did it. Why?"

"I will never forget the way she looked at me," Nina said.

"Oh, my child. My father felt that he too had no choice. As a good Christian, he had to do what he could to save God's Chosen People."

"But how, with all the food shortages, did you feed all the people who took refuge in your house?"

"You know, we wondered that too. But father would say, 'The Lord will provide.' And every day, when we awakened, there would be a basket of food before our door."

"The ten Booms were good Christians," Nina concluded, "and because that was true, Corrie's father and sister died.

"Elwood, I think often about them—and how, while the world stood silent as 6 million perished, a simple watchmaker could feel so deeply."

As the plaques along The Street of Righteous Gentiles testify, the ten Booms were not alone in feeling so deeply for suffering Jews.

Carolina Taitz and the Micko Family

Carolina Taitz found her "hiding place" with the family of Vladimir Micko, a Christian evangelist who removed some of the floorboards of his home and dug out a shelter for his Jewish houseguest.

Carolina had been driven out of her home in the Riga Ghetto in Latvia at 4:30 one morning in November 1941. Ghetto inhabitants were herded into the nearby Rumbuli Forest and commanded to halt. "We could see," she said, "that a mass grave had already been dug for us. We were told to undress. People screamed. I will never forget the snow mixed with blood, the children who were shot....

Naked, the people were shot by machine-gun fire and fell into the grave." Her last-moment deliverance came when a Nazi officer called for women who could sew to raise their hands. Carolina was among the fortunate ones.

She eventually arrived at the Mickos' door in a desperate attempt to escape the Nazis before she was killed. For the Mickos, there was no other choice. She was welcomed into their home. For three years, until she was liberated in 1944, Carolina lived with the family.

"The whole family accepted me immediately and surrounded me with love. They cared for me as a member of the family and never demanded any payment or monetary reward for their kindness. Without their selfless love, their courage, and their humane actions, I would never have survived."

Vladimir, the evangelist, seemed to be a man possessed with an inordinate amount of courage. To gain entrance into the ghetto, he sewed a yellow Jewish star on his coat. His boldness frightened Carolina, and she warned him against taking such risks. Nevertheless, he went into the ghetto often to take to her relatives and others bread, sugar, butter, cheese, and anything else he could lay his hands on. Carolina thought it truly a divine miracle that the Nazis did not recognize him.

David and the Baptists

David Prital, from the city of Lutsk in the Ukraine, was in dire straits as he tried to stay one step ahead of the Germans. Then it was somehow brought to his mind that back home, before the war, the family's maid had been a Baptist. David fondly recalled her piety and her love for the Jewish people. Her devotion stood out against the anti-Semitism that was so much a part of life in the Ukraine.

Bolstered by his memories, he decided to seek out

some Baptists and see if they would give him shelter. A Polish peasant he met outside a small village directed him to a nearby farm owned by a Baptist family. After briefly conversing with the farmer, Ivan Jaciuk, outside the house, the Jewish youth was led through the door.

"God has brought us an important guest," Ivan informed his family. "Come, let us thank the Lord."

The farmer and his wife fell to their knees, praising God for having granted them the privilege of meeting a son of Israel and imploring Him to save the remnant of Jews who were hiding in the fields and forests. David could hardly believe his ears.

He was even more impressed when, over dinner, his host said to him, "Try to understand; I too am Jewish. Spiritually, I am a Jew, and this encounter with you gives me a lot to think about, because it verifies the prophet's word that a saving remnant will be spared."

David's stay at Ivan's farm was, by necessity, limited because his neighbor was a rabid Jew-hater. But Ivan took David to another Baptist family, who sheltered him as long as they safely could, then passed him on to yet another Baptist family. The Baptist-to-Baptist hospitality chain was extended to David until he joined a partisan band in the forest.

One of the young Jew's fondest memories of his time among the Baptists was on a day when he found himself in particularly low spirits. The Baptist peasant with whom he was staying sat down beside him.

"I see you are sad and depressed. Allow me to sing you a song that will strengthen your spirit." Then, in the original Hebrew, he began to chant Psalm 126. "When the LORD turned again the captivity of Zion, we were like them that dream. Then was our mouth filled with laughter, and our tongue with singing; then said they among the nations, The LORD hath done great things for them. The

LORD hath done great things for us, whereof we are glad."

André Trocmé

A French pastor, André Trocmé, was deeply involved in helping the Jewish people. At one point he was asked by the authorities to give them a list of the Jews in town who were living under assumed names. He replied, "Even if I had such a list, I would not pass it on to you. These people have come seeking aid and protection. I am therefore their pastor, their shepherd. The shepherd does not betray the sheep in his keeping."

On another occasion he was confronted about his obvious association with Jews. "Jews?" he said; "I don't know what a Jew is. I only know human beings."

André Trocmé, under interrogation by the Gestapo, admitted his role in sheltering Jewish children. His reply was straightforward: "I defend the weak." For defending the weak he was sent to the Buchenwald concentration camp, where he died in 1944.

Gerardus Pontier

Shlomo and his brother Hanan were walking along a Dutch street when a cyclist, noticing their yellow stars, stopped to ask how they were faring in those hard times. "We could be sent to the concentration camp any day," Shlomo replied. "God only knows what will happen to us and our family."

Pastor Gerardus Pontier gave the boys his address and told them to contact him if they were notified of an impending move to the camp. That day came, and the boys and their family found themselves at the pastor's door.

The pastor greeted them warmly, then went inside to get his wife Dora. Standing side by side with tears in their eyes, they told Shlomo and his family that they would be welcome guests in their home. "Don't worry, my child. We have made a decision, and God will protect us. Son of Israel, we are happy to give you any help. It is the duty of every Christian to help those in danger."

Pastor Pontier would later find danger of his own when he was arrested by the Gestapo for underground activities. He was sent to Scheveningen prison.

Jan Gort

I suppose if we looked for a statement to sum up the attitude of the Christians who defied the Nazis and jeopardized their lives for Jewish people, it would be found in the words of Jan Gort. Jan and his wife Emma were Dutch Christians who had hidden Jewish children during the war. They were in Jerusalem in 1977 to plant a tree in the Garden of the Righteous at Yad Vashem.

Just before the ceremony began, a small Jewish boy walked up to Gort, took his hand, and said, "Thank you." Deeply touched, the guardian of Jewish children told how he and Emma found the inner strength they needed. "We kept in mind the words of Queen Esther when she went to King Ahasuerus: 'If I perish, I perish' [Esther 4:16]. And those of our redeemer, who said, 'Whosoever will save his life shall lose it, and whosoever will lose his life for my sake shall find it' [Matthew 16:25]. And God did protect us. 'A thousand shall fall at thy side, and ten thousand at thy right hand, but it shall not come near thee' [Psalm 91:7]."

"If I perish, I perish." That word of absolute commitment is what drove so many of the Jan and Emma Dorts of the Holocaust years to do what they knew, before God, was the right thing.

Never Forget

A year ago I walked The Street of the Righteous Gentiles with a longtime Polish friend who had survived the Holocaust. Like so many others, Zvi lost his entire family in the maelstrom that was World War II.

"Zvi, how does it feel for you to come here?" I asked.

"Well, the feeling is not so good. It brings it all back, like it was yesterday."

"And your family? Do you think of them here?"

"Not only here, at this place, Elwood. I think of them every day. They are never out of my thoughts."

"When you walk among so many terrible memories, how do you feel toward those who were responsible for so much suffering?"

"I can say this, and I do not say it lightly. Now, as a believer, I can forgive. But I can never, never forget."

Prior to the release of *Schindler's List*, I was invited by the Israeli ambassador to attend a private screening in Washington D.C. It was quite moving to view the film with an audience made up almost entirely of Jewish people and to experience their reactions to what was being shown. For the most part, the evening was marked by what I would call a kind of heavy silence, broken from time to time by the sobs of those too deeply affected to control their emotions.

As the story unfolded, it occurred to me that there were probably few Jewish people in the theater that night who could not name immediate family members, relatives, or friends who had died in the Holocaust.

In the final scene, in an expertly crafted way, Steven Spielberg had some of the actual survivors, who had been portrayed by actors in the film, walk in a line past the grave of Oskar Schindler, which is on Mount Zion in Jerusalem. As they passed, each one placed a memorial stone atop the slab covering Schindler's grave. You can see these stones on graves and at military memorials all over Israel. They are placed by people out of love and with respect for the memory of persons dear to them.

Cut into the stone containing the inscription on Schindler's grave was a large cross. For me, the sight of Jewish people—Holocaust survivors—placing stones of respect beside a Christian cross said a great deal. While I am not a person particularly given to symbolism and display, as I looked at that cross and those stones, I was filled with emotion.

I once wrote an article for *Moody* magazine entitled "When the Cross Becomes a Sword." Too often, regrettably, the cross has been beaten into a sword by perpetrators of evil.

But such was not the case in this scene. Spielberg, to his credit, showed us the quality that should consistently dominate the relationship between evangelical Christians and the Jewish community. And it shouldn't take a Holocaust to make it happen.

4

The Evangelicals

The late Rabbi Meir Kahane, founder of the militant Jewish Defense League and later, in Israel, of the controversial Kach political party, was not fond of evangelical Christians. He did, however, possess the insight to discern that what had taken place among evangelicals had revolutionized their thinking about Jewish people and Israel.

"Israel has," he said in an article titled "Christians for Zion," "within the United States a weapon that itself believes in and can convince others that the United States' true interest is total and unconditional backing of the Jewish State....I refer to the tens of fundamentalist and evangelical Christian Protestant sects, whose members number in the millions and whose leaders have national and international influence....These are groups who are totally Bible oriented, who believe that the Bible is the literal word of God and to whom the literal prophecies of a return to Zion by the Jewish people and the setting up of a Jewish State are absolute preconditions for the final redemption" (*The Jewish Press*, January 24, 1975).

Rabbi Kahane, who was later gunned down by radical Muslims in New York City, saw clearly the remarkable trends that are now facts of life in Israel and among a significant number of Christians in the Western world.

Over the past few centuries, thoughts and actions have emerged that cannot be ignored. They are so revolutionary that together they have changed the face of both Christianity and Judaism and in the process altered the map of the world. That these took place in close relationship to each other, yet as distinctly separate entities, makes the phenomenon all the more intriguing. Simply put, we are dealing with two returns: one in the realm of Christian theology, the other in the world of the Jew.

A Return to Biblical Thinking

There is today a new dialogue taking place among Jews and Christians. Dr. Harry Hurwitz, former Minister of Information at the Israeli Embassy in Washington D.C. and adviser to former Israeli Prime Ministers Begin and Shamir, refers to it as the common ground occupied by "Bible-believing Christians and Bible-believing Jews." The common ground that Hurwitz speaks of relates to Israel. At the heart of his statement are the words "Bible-believing." He is defining the relationship between biblically driven Christian and Jewish Zionists.

Christians should not be turned off by the word *Zionist*, which has in the halls of the United Nations and among conspiracy-hunting fanatics been given a bad name. At its root, Zionism simply means *a commitment to the inherent right of the Jewish people to have an internationally recognized homeland in the Middle East*—the place referred to by

Jews today as "Eretz Israel." Whether or not people consciously utter the word about themselves, if they accept the concept of a biblically endorsed Jewish right to the land, they are Zionists.

The True Christian Roots

During the first two centuries of the Christian era, the church was predominantly premillennial; it taught that the Messiah would literally fulfill prophecies related to His second coming and establish a thousand-year kingdom reign on the earth before the eternal state begins. The theology was based on a literal interpretation of clear biblical propositions from both the Old and New Testaments.

For example, when Christ referred to the coming kingdom, His disciples understood Him to mean an earthly, messianic reign. Following His resurrection, He was queried about the matter by His inner circle of followers. Acts 1:3 tells us, "To whom [the apostles] also he showed himself alive after his passion by many infallible proofs, being seen by them forty days, and speaking of the things pertaining to the kingdom of God." Their response was to the point: "When they therefore were come together, they asked of him, saying, Lord, wilt thou at this time restore again the kingdom to Israel?" His answer: "It is not for you to know the times or the seasons, which the Father hath put in his own power" (Acts 1:6,7).

His instruction, their question, and His answer all related to the kingdom that God through the prophets had promised to Israel—a literal reign by the Messiah as the legitimate heir to the throne of David.

Romans 11 embellishes the theme in a way that those who deny a literal prophetic future for the nation of Israel are hardpressed to explain away: "I [the apostle Paul] say then, Hath God cast away his people? God forbid. For I also am an Israelite, of the seed of Abraham, of the tribe of Benjamin. God hath not cast away his people whom he foreknew" (Romans 11:1,2a).

After a thorough discussion of the relative positions of Jews and Christian Gentiles in this dispensation (to which we shall refer later), Paul returned to Israel's national, kingdom destiny.

"And so," he affirmed, "all Israel shall be saved; as it is written, There shall come out of Zion the Deliverer, and shall turn away ungodliness from Jacob" (Romans 11:26). The quotation is taken from Isaiah 59:20: "The Redeemer shall come to Zion, and unto those who turn from transgression in Jacob." These references are unmistakably related to a coming national reconciliation of Israel to the promised Messiah-Deliverer. In fact, verse 20 begins a paragraph running well into Isaiah chapter 60 that conveys some marvelous aspects of the coming kingdom. Its primary features are:

1. The King will reign: "the LORD shall arise upon thee, and his glory shall be seen upon thee" (60:2).
2. The nations will pay homage to Him: "the nations shall come to thy light, and kings to the brightness of thy rising" (60:3).
3. Israel will be regathered: "Who are these that fly like a cloud, and like the doves to their windows?" (60:8)—the final ingathering of the exiles.

As previously mentioned, for its first two centuries of existence, the Christian church adhered largely to the literal kingdom concept. However, in the last ten years of the second century, a radical change took place. The heretical school of theology at Alexandria, Egypt, developed a principle of interpretation proposing that the Bible should be understood in a nonliteral or allegorical sense.

Augustine (354-430) rescued the church from central elements of this heresy. Strangely enough, however, the move away from allegory was not applied to prophetic areas of the Scriptures. Even the Protestant Reformation failed to encourage a return to a more literal view of interpreting the prophetic portions, which make up approximately one-third of the Bible.

This approach became known as *amillennialism*—no literal kingdom for Israel. Amillennialism, which continues to be the majority view of the church, for the most part adheres to the Augustinian interpretation regarding prophecy. This relates the millennium only to the present age as a spiritual kingdom ruling in the hearts of Christians or embodied in the progress of the gospel through the church. In other words, the church has now become Israel, and all that God promised to Abraham and his posterity has been spiritualized and placed in the coffers of the church.

Incidentally, virtually all liberal theologians endorse the amillennial position.

Premillennialists hold an entirely different view on matters touching prophecy and Israel. A basic reason for this is found in a simple examination of what the Bible and past history have to say. Approximately half of the prophecies in the Bible have already been fulfilled, and all of them in a literal way, leading to the conclusion that unfulfilled prophecies will likewise be fulfilled literally.

Interestingly, all orthodox Christians, whether amillennial or premillennial, believe and teach that prophecy related to the first coming of Christ was fulfilled literally and in minutely accurate detail. Thus what the Old Testament messianic Scriptures declared was understood and interpreted as would be any other document in the normal sense of interpretation.

To premillennialists it seems totally illogical that amillennialists can accept the literal fulfillment of the first-coming prophecies but insist on spiritualizing second-coming prophecies that are presented in exactly the same way as the first-coming prophecies. This seems to represent a sort of theological schizophrenia. What is left, in such a scheme of things, to the future of the Jewish people and their nation? Would it be too harsh to say that stripping the nation of all its unrescinded promises represents a benign form of theological anti-Semitism?

We must point out that there are number of variations in details of both amillenial and premillennial views. However, for our purpose in this book, we will look only at the central differences between the two, particularly with regard to Israel. The perspective presented in this book is that of evangelical premillennialism.

Neither British Nor Israel

There is another view that deserves comment. It is a belief system outside the realm of either premillennial or ammillennial interpretation, both of which fit generally into the category of orthodox Christian belief. While both of the views mentioned above involve theological interpretation, the system called *British Israelism* involves physical and nationalistic aspirations. It is important to consider this view because it has spawned a number of cults, some of which pose a serious physical threat to the Jewish people. This system also actively opposes a Jewish role for Israel.

It is a matter of serious concern to Jews and Christians that most militant anti-Semites operating today adopt some form of British Israelism.

British-Israelism, or Anglo-Israelism, came into existence slightly more than a hundred years ago. An Englishman named Richard Brothers originated this method of biblical interpretation, which promotes the idea that Anglo-Saxon peoples are in fact Israel.

Consequently they are the true heirs of all divine promises to the Jewish nation.

The movement reached its zenith when the British Empire held sway over a sprawling colonial system, engendering a considerable amount of imperial-sized pride in some quarters. Credulous religionists saw in Anglo-Israelism an answer to the perplexing question of what to do with the vast repository of biblical promises to Israel. To their way of thinking, it was apparent that the Jewish people were in no position to expect a literal fulfillment of their aspirations for a land and a kingdom.

As the British Empire became frayed and the balance of world power shifted to the United States, Anglo-Israelism was popularized in this country. A primary figure in its rise here was the late Herbert W. Armstrong, with his "World of Tomorrow" radio broadcasts and *The Plain Truth* magazine.

British-Israelism was constructed on four postulates.

1. The ten northern tribes of Israel were deported by the Assyrians in 721 B.C. and were subsequently lost—*the ten lost tribes*. According to advocate Armstrong, "When the southern kingdom of Judah was taken into captivity by Nebuchadnezzar of Babylon, the Assyrians migrated northwest— and the ten-tribed Israelites with them! Utterly lost. They were utterly gone! They were lost from view." As the Assyrian Empire declined, "Israel" wandered westward across northern Europe. Later these people became the Saxe, or Sythians, who moved through Europe to invade England as the Saxon people.

2. Henceforth the British would be identified as Israelitish Ephraim, with the fledgling United States installed as Manasseh. In this scheme of

things, David's throne was transferred from Jerusalem to England. This caused one enthusiast, Hermon L. Hoeh, to proclaim, "Elizabeth II actually sits on the throne of King David of Israel."

3. Israel (the ten northern tribes) is forever to be distinguished from Jews (the house of Judah), which has been left under a permanent curse. That curse emanated from the idea that it was Judah and Levi who put Christ to death, while saying, "His blood be on us and on our children" (Matthew 27:25).

4. All the divine promises to Israel find fruition in God's blessings upon England and America.

This hodgepodge of ideas is historically and biblically proven preposterous. The ten tribes were never lost. Biblical references to specific representatives of the ten tribes crop up repeatedly in both the Old and New Testaments. Here are two obvious examples.

At King Hezekiah's invitation, Jews from the northern kingdom settled in Judah. His call to attend the Passover in Jerusalem went out to the people "throughout all Israel and Judah," with a special word for those "who are escaped out of the hand of the kings of Assyria." Reference is made to responses from five of the northern tribes: Ephraim, Manasseh, Zebulun, Asher, and Issachar (2 Chronicles 30).

When Josiah led a religious revival nearly a century after the Assyrian deportations, gifts were sent to Jerusalem. "And when they came to Hilkiah, the high priest, they delivered the money that was brought into the house of God, which the Levites who kept the doors had gathered of the hand of Manasseh and Ephraim, and of all the remnant of Israel" (2 Chronicles 34:9). Thus Ephraim and Manasseh were not in the process of settling down in England and America; they were at home in Israel.

In his book *Kingdom of the Cults*, Walter Martin repudiates the claim by proponents of British-Israelism that the terms *Israel* and *Jews* or *Judah* are never used synonymously in the Bible, but that *Israel* always refers to the ten northern tribes and *Jews* or *Judah* are exclusively the southern tribes. "After the Babylonian captivity," Martin writes, "from which the Jews returned, Ezra records the remnant were called by the name of Jews eight times, and by the name Israel forty times. Nehemiah records eleven times they are Jews, and proceeds to describe them as Israel twenty-two times."

The New Testament is no less emphatic. Acts 2 alone refers to "Jews" (verse 5), "men of Judea" (verse 14), and "men of Israel" (verse 22). To cap it off, Peter in his sermon on Pentecost in Jerusalem addressed himself to "all the house of Israel" (verse 36).

Thus the proponents of British-Israelism have put together a tottering house of cards promoting the superiority of race and people. Like the infamous *Protocols of the Elders of Zion*, although repeatedly exposed for what it is, British-Israelism persists as a tool in the hands of anti-Semites who wish to do intellectual or physical violence to Jewry.

Giving Israel Her Due

The resurgence of premillennial thinking among a significant number of evangelical Christians over the past few centuries has brought to the scene a consistent approach to interpretation of prophetic Scriptures. The great boon for Bible students found in the premillennial view is that it makes the prophetic Scriptures comprehensible and world events decipherable.

A central factor in premillennial interpretation is not to misidentify God's program for Israel with His program for the church. Some of the greatest confusion in Bible teaching arises when such misidentification occurs.

Scripture's teaching about Israel is one of the great assurances that the book we call the Bible is historically accurate—a trustworthy document that only a God who sees the future before it is lived out on the stage of human history could produce. Let's take a text from Scripture and see how history comes alongside the written Word. The passage is Ezekiel 11:16-20.

> Thus saith the Lord GOD: Although I have cast them far off among the nations, and although I have scattered them among the countries, yet will I be to them a little sanctuary in the countries where they shall come.... Thus saith the Lord GOD: I will even gather you from the people, and assemble you out of the countries where ye have been scattered, and I will give you the land of Israel. And they shall come there, and they shall take away all its detestable things and all its abominations from there. *And I will give them one heart,* and I will put a new spirit within you; and I will take the stony heart out of their flesh, and will give them a heart of flesh, that they may walk in my statutes and keep my ordinances, and do them; *and they shall be my people, and I will be their God.*

Four essentials are defined in this passage. (These same things are said in different words in a number of other passages.) First, we are told that Israel would be cast among the nations. We need not be reminded that this is one of the best–attested facts in all of human history. For nearly 2000 years, Jews have wandered as footsore sojourners among often–inhospitable Gentiles. The prophecies of Israel's dispersion have been very literally fulfilled.

Next is the promise that even though the nation would be forced from its home for extended periods of time, there would always be an Israel. That Jewry has survived, as the Scriptures said it would, is certainly one of the great miracles of human history. Every rational conclusion would insist on the assimilation of the Jew, especially given the vilification faced in virtually every society they entered. However, the Lord promised to be "a little sanctuary" to them, implying protection and a limit to how long their suffering and expulsion would last. So emphatic are the Scriptures about the divine protection of the Jew and the nation that Jeremiah 31:35-37 lays down an astonishing declaration of intent by God to preserve His Chosen People.

> Thus saith the LORD, who giveth the sun for a light by day and the ordinances of the moon and of the stars for a light by night, who divideth the sea when its waves roar; the LORD of hosts is his name: If those ordinances depart from before me, saith the LORD, then the seed of Israel also shall cease from being a nation before me forever. Thus saith the LORD, If heaven above can be measured and the foundations of the earth searched out beneath, I will also cast off all the seed of Israel for all that they have done, saith the LORD.

In other words, if anyone is to destroy Israel, he must control the universe and dethrone God Himself. Thus in a very real sense the credibility of the Bible is placed squarely on the pedestal of Jewish preservation—a remarkable concept indeed. The Scriptures have stated it prophetically; history is proving it literally.

Third, the nation would one day be brought back to Israel, the land of their fathers. Biblically, two movements are involved, and one seems to be well under way. The resurrection of the modern State of Israel has been a *once-in-the history-of-the-planet* event, and many of us have stood in awe of the spectacle. Jews from some 108 nations have streamed into the land since the turn of the century. In the latest eruption of returnees to the ancient land from the former Soviet Union, nearly half a million Jews have gone home. Such numbers are truly astonishing. I wonder how many of us realize that to find anything comparable to the return of the Jews from Russia we would have to go as far back as the days of Moses and Pharaoh and those famous "Let my people go" confrontations. Yes, the Scriptures said there would be an eventual secular return of the Jewish people to Israel, and today we are witnessing it historically.

Finally, Ezekiel 11 announces the climactic reconciliation of the nation to the Messiah and the subsequent golden age of His triumphant reign. He will be their God and they will be His people. This is the consummation of His plan for His special people. Only this aspect has not yet been literally fulfilled. But considering what has transpired regarding the other prophetic projections, can we expect less than a literal fulfillment?

A Promised Land for a Chosen People

The broad view of evangelical premillennial belief about Israel is based on the following biblically rooted propositions.

Genesis 12:1-3 introduces the basic provisions of God's covenant with Israel.

> Now the LORD had said unto Abram, Get thee out of thy country and from thy kindred and from thy father's house unto a land that I will show thee; and I will make of thee a great

nation, and I will bless thee and make thy
name great, and thou shalt be a blessing. And
I will bless them that bless thee and curse him
that curseth thee; and in thee shall all families
of the earth be blessed.

This passage establishes land rights (to be detailed
later) and the promise that the presence of Abram and his
posterity would bless the world; it also sets forth the principle of individual and international relationships with
Abram's seed.

Genesis 12:7 adds an indispensable note: "And the
LORD appeared unto Abram and said, Unto thy seed will
I give this land...." Dr. John Walvoord, an eminent premillennial scholar, has emphasized the importance of this
statement. "It is not too much to say that the interpretation of Genesis 12:7 determines, in large measure, the
prophetic interpretation of the rest of the Bible" (*Prophecy
Knowledge Handbook*, p. 26).

It is fascinating to note that the land grant for a Jewish
homeland envisioned in the Balfour Declaration possesses
borders similar to those outlined in the Bible.

Genesis 15:18 delineates the boundaries of the land
promised to Abram. "In the same day the LORD made a
covenant with Abram, saying, Unto thy seed have I given
this land, from the river of Egypt unto the great river, the
river Euphrates."

Abraham, however, had two sons. Who then would
become the principal heir of the covenant? God answered
that question in Genesis 17. "And God said, Sarah, thy
wife, shall bear thee a son indeed, and thou shalt call his
name Isaac; and I will establish my covenant with him for
an everlasting covenant, and with his seed after him"
(Genesis 17:19).

So the line of descent was established through Isaac—
that is, through the people known to us as Jews.

But at the center of one of the most volatile contests on earth today is the question of who holds the rights to the land called Israel. There are those who charge Jews and Christians (who say that the land has been given to the Jewish people in perpetuity because it is theirs by divine right) with being anti-Arab and discriminating against the sons of Ishmael. The following verses in Genesis 17, however, speak to that very issue.

"And as for Ishmael, I have heard thee: Behold, I have blessed him and will make him fruitful, and will multiply him exceedingly; twelve princes shall he beget, and I will make him a great nation. But my covenant will I establish with Isaac, whom Sarah shall bear unto thee at this set time in the next year" (Genesis 17:20,21).

There is no inkling of discrimination to be found here. As a matter of simple fact, the land holdings of the Arab peoples today far exceed that granted to Israel. Israel's current difficulty is keeping the small slice of the Promised Land it now holds.

What we learn from these foundational passages is that land rights for Israel are, from a biblical viewpoint, nonnegotiable. Whether the Jewish people are in or out of their land at any particular juncture in history is irrelevant. Eretz Israel belongs to the Jewish people. This fact impacts evangelicals in such a way that there is unqualified support among this sizable segment of the Christian community for Israel's presence and national rights in the Middle East. When Israelis identify such evangelical Christians as Israel's best friends in the Gentile world, it is not a statement to be taken lightly. Evangelical allegiance does not shift with every political wind that blows. It is based on a commitment stemming from the Word of God as we understand it.

Furthermore, Jewish people as individuals (and as a whole, for that matter) are to be recognized for who they are—God's Chosen People—and not only for who they are, but for what they contribute to the general well-being of the peoples of the earth. More will be said of this later, but for Christians the biblically mandated view of the Jew is one of appreciation, support, and willingness to be true friends.

The idea of being the Chosen People rankles some of my Jewish friends. A short time ago one said that Jews, he supposed, were legitimately designated the "Chosen People." "But I'll tell you how I feel about it personally. I wouldn't mind terribly if God decided to choose someone else for a while. This being the 'Chosen People' is a pretty tough job." Nonetheless, the assignment has been made by a higher authority than either Jews or Christians; ours is to respect the title and act accordingly.

Another issue is anti-Semitism. If God regards those who defame and persecute Abraham's heirs as worthy of being cursed, we have a binding obligation to combat anti-Semitism wherever it is manifested. This is one vital area where Jews and evangelicals are obligated to present a united front.

Jacob's Trouble

The one significant issue not touched upon in the foregoing discussion of basic evangelical beliefs is that of a time of great trouble in Israel's future. This, by the way, is not an idea born of Christian minds less than appreciative of Jewish people. Rather, it is one birthed in the Scriptures, and we have certainly been exposed to harbingers of this period throughout Jewish history.

Jeremiah 30:5-9 is one among many portions of Scripture describing this subject. I choose it because it succinctly states the primary issues of the period.

"Thus saith the LORD, We have heard a voice of trembling, of fear, and not of peace....Alas! for that day is great, so that none is like it; it is even the time of Jacob's trouble, but he shall be saved out of it. For it shall come to pass in that day, saith the LORD of hosts, that I will break his yoke from off thy neck, and will burst thy bonds, and strangers shall no more enslave them, but they shall serve the LORD their God...."

This brief but intense era seems to epitomize the age-old conflict of darkness and light, of good and evil, and the transcending Satan-God struggle. From all indications in Scripture and substantiating historic evidence, this period will embody the last attempt at Holocaust against the Jewish nation. It seems to involve the supreme marshaling of anti-Semitic hordes against Jewry and God Himself.

Beyond that dark horizon, however, is a brightness unparalleled in the history of the Jewish people—or the world, for that matter. "But he shall be saved out of it," the prophet says reassuringly. I personally, am fascinated by the words chosen by the God-given authors of the Bible in describing the climax of this troubled time.

- "He [Israel] shall be saved out of it" (Jeremiah 30:7).
- "The Redeemer shall come to Zion" (Isaiah 59:20).
- "I...will refine them [Israel] as silver is refined" (Zechariah 13:9).
- "Then shall the LORD go forth and fight against those nations, as when he fought in the day of battle" (Zechariah 14:3).
- "I [God] will say, It is my people; and they shall say, The LORD is my God" (Zechariah 13:9).

These are just a few selections that tell of Israel's salvation out of Jacob's trouble, its reconciliation with the Messiah, its refining as a nation destined to be God's unique witness to the nations, its protection by His mighty hand, and its uniting with Him forever.

The idea of a time of trouble for Israel before the coming of the Messiah is not confined to Christian end-time theology. Jewish sources also espouse the concept. The book *Mashiach—Principle of Mashiach and the Messianic Era in Jewish Law and Tradition* by Jacob Immanuel Schochet (quoting sources from the Midrash) records the following.

The Time Immediately Before Mashiach

The time appointed by G-d for the Messianic redemption is a closely guarded secret.[8] Nonetheless, we are offered many hints to recognize its proximity: when certain conditions come about, await the imminent coming of Mashiach.

Most of these conditions are quite disturbing, clearly displaying a situation of the very "bottom of the pit."[9] One major source describes the world-condition as follows: increase in insolence and impudence; oppressing inflation; unbridled irresponsibility on the part of authorities; centers of learning will turn into bawdy houses; wars; many destitutes begging, with none to pity them; wisdom shall be putrid; the pious shall be despised; truth will be abandoned; the young will insult the old; family breakup with mutual recriminations; impudent leadership.[10]

Other sources add: lack of scholars; succession of troubles and evil decrees; famines; mutual denunciations; epidemics of terrible diseases; poverty and scarcity; cursing and blaspheming; international confrontations—nations provoking and fighting each other.[11] In short, it will be a time of suffering that will make it look like G-d is asleep. These are the birth-pangs of the Mashiach, bearable only in anticipation of the bliss that follows them.

"When you see a generation ever dwindling, hope for him...when you see a generation overwhelmed by many troubles as by a river, await him."[12] "When you see nations fighting each other, look toward the feet of the Machiach."[13]

Little wonder that some sages expressed apprehensions about those days in terms of, "Let the [Mashiach] come, but let me not see him."[14] The prevailing attitude, however, is to await his coming in spite of it all....

All of this is in preparation for the magnificent era of the millennium previously mentioned, that time when "the LORD shall be king over all the earth; and in that day shall there be one LORD, and his name one" (Zechariah 14:9).

Of all the portions of the Bible speaking of this glorious time held dear by believing Jews and Christians, perhaps one says it best. Addressing the final ingathering of the exiles and subsequent events, Isaiah says:

Surely the coasts shall wait for me, and the ships of Tarshish first, to bring thy sons from far, their silver and their gold with them, unto the name of the LORD thy God, and to the Holy One of Israel, because he hath glorified thee. And the sons of foreigners shall build up thy walls, and their kings shall minister unto thee, for in my wrath I smote thee, but in my favor have I had mercy on thee (Isaiah 60:9,10).

After centuries of dispersion and unwarranted vilification, followed by decades of an agonizing search for peace, at long last true peace will come—the kind that the

Jewish people have longed for over the centuries and the millennia. They will no longer be regarded as a pariah among the nations. Rather, Israel will be regarded as a partner whom the nations of the world will be happy to join in building up the walls of Jerusalem and the cities of the Promised Land.

I have been captivated for years by those statements in the Old Testament that speak of the time when the animosity between Israel and predatory Gentile nations will be no more. One of the most compelling of these verses touching this issue is found in Zechariah.

> Yea, many peoples and strong nations shall come to seek the LORD of hosts in Jerusalem, and to pray before the LORD. Thus saith the LORD of hosts: In those days it shall come to pass that ten men shall take hold out of all languages of the nations, even shall take hold of the skirt of him that is a Jew, saying, We will go with you, for we have heard that God is with you (Zechariah 8:22,23).

We stand in awe before the great finale to Zechariah, which has so much to say about the future destiny of Israel and the nations. The final scene portrays the nations of the world making annual pilgrimages to Jerusalem for the Feast of Tabernacles: "It shall come to pass that everyone that is left of all the nations which came against Jerusalem shall even go up from year to year to worship the King, the LORD of hosts, and to keep the feast of tabernacles" (Zechariah 14:16).

Evangelical Christians who have joined in the return to biblical roots read the Bible in the full cultural, historic, and prophetic context in which it was cast. In so doing we recognize all that the Scriptures reveal about Israel and its people. We have a firm grasp on historic reality, and Israel has gained millions of true friends.

In all honesty, we acknowledge that the central issue standing between Christians and Jews at this point is the identity of the Messiah. You may have noticed that the climactic Scriptures regarding Israel's future destiny have at their center the Messiah reigning over His redeemed and regathered nation.

Jerusalem's former mayor, the venerable Teddy Kolleck, once made a fascinating statement about the identity of the Messiah, one that pretty well sums up our diverse positions.

"I have the hardest job in the world," Mayor Kolleck said, "to prepare Jerusalem for the Messiah. When he comes, I will respectfully ask him, 'Sir, have you been to this place before?'" That is indeed the question. We Christians believe it has been answered for us, while many in Israel are still seeking their Messiah.

The return to biblical roots by many evangelicals has brought a dramatic change in their attitude toward the Jewish people and the nation of Israel. In practical terms, it has made a tremendous contribution to the Christian and Jewish communities and has done much to help evangelicals speak out against anti-Jewish bias found even among some professing Christians.

Anti-Semitism is sometimes difficult for some Christians to comprehend—that is, the street-level hostility that Jewish people face daily, even in the United States. Many times it is not frontal but subtle—something that Jewish people must sense, even though nothing has been said. We all, for example, have heard complaints about the Jews' determination not to allow the world to forget the Holocaust, or that Jewish people have the reputation of "sticking together and looking after one another"—an attribute that happens to be a virtue Jesus demands of Christians.

A Place to Hide

I was given some pointed insights into these attitudes few years ago while interviewing a Jewish senator who is from a rather prominent family. We talked at length about his personal experiences. He told me that even though his family's business was well-known and made a significant contribution to the community, they were refused membership in some civic organizations. He recalled once applying for membership in a prestigious country club, only to be turned down because he was Jewish.

After we discussed these and other more serious affronts, the senator turned the conversation toward some of his fears about the future. "I'm very concerned," he said. "What we're seeing now in some of the hate groups has caused me to do some serious thinking. And I can tell you that I am not alone when it comes to being apprehensive about what may lie ahead.

"When you come right down to it, I suppose there are times when every Jew, whether he expresses it openly or not, looks around at his circle of friends and poses a crucial question: If an Adolf Hitler were to come to power here in America, who among these people would give me a place to hide?"

Whenever I read or hear of some ugly story of swastikas smeared on synagogue walls, or Jewish cemeteries being desecrated, or the rantings of haters about "blood-sucking Jews," I remember my conversation with the senator. I wonder if he is not now even more aware of his question and vulnerability. I'm sure many other Jewish people are.

For Christians, this brings to the fore the responsibility faced by the courageous shielders of Holocaust victims whose stories we heard in the preceding chapter. One day we may have our turn at demonstrating our care for and solidarity with the people who are so close to God's heart.

I came across a touching illustration of such care and concern a few years ago while speaking about the Jewish people and Israel at a church in Michigan. During one of my addresses I mentioned my interview with the senator. I then urged the congregation to relate their appreciation for what Jewish people had given us all, and in practical ways I encouraged them to demonstrate genuine concern for Israel and their Jewish friends.

A year later I returned to that church. One of the first people to approach me was a young woman eager to tell me her story.

"Do you remember the story you told when you were here last year, the one about the Jewish senator?"

"Certainly," I replied.

"I left that meeting determined to tell my Jewish employer about my personal concerns and support as a Christian for the Jewish people. We had worked together for several years, but I had never been able to bring myself to say anything to him.

"On Monday morning, as I entered the office, I met him in the aisle on the way to my desk.

" 'Good morning,' he said.

"By the look on my face, he must have thought I had something to say.

" 'Is something on your mind?' he asked.

"My mind suddenly went blank. The little speech I had prepared was completely gone.

"I looked at him for a moment and then just blurted it out. 'I just want you to know that if an Adolf Hitler ever comes to America, I will give you a place to hide.' "

The man was so moved by her startling declaration that he broke down and wept. They both wept—and well they did, because many of us fear that we are perhaps entering a period in history when evangelical Christians, as well as Jews, may be looking for a place to hide.

5

The Evangelical Agenda

The elderly gentleman was courtly and had an easy way of carrying on a conversation. To me he looked a little like humorist Victor Borge. *Well,* I thought, as we waited for the EL AL jumbo jet to receive that last rush of passengers, *at least I'll have a pleasant fellow to chat with on the long flight to Tel Aviv.*

It wasn't to be, however, because soon the flight attendant was asking my companion if he would mind changing seats with a young, agitated Hasidic Jew whose original seat assignment was in the middle of a group of about a dozen Catholic nuns. My friend obliged, hauling his carry-on luggage from beneath the seat and the overhead compartment.

Not long after he had settled in, the flight attendant was back. This time she courteously asked the row of nuns, along with the Borge look-alike, if they would mind giving way to a family whose father was rather loudly insisting that his contingent be seated together. Once again the carry-ons came out, and the man moved up the aisle, scanning the numbers for his newly assigned seat.

He arrived and put his things away just in time to be confronted by another vexation. This time he was asked to make way for a husband and wife who had inadvertently been separated when seats were assigned. Once more he went through the now-familiar exit process and sauntered down the aisle toward his new destination. As he passed my seat, shaking his head rather dolefully, he said, "You know, sometimes it is very hard to be a Jew." The patient fellow must have thought he was sampling the wanderings of the Diaspora.

I have thought about him from time to time when some of our Jewish friends have had trouble understanding why so many evangelical Christians care about Jewish people and go out of their way to demonstrate unconditional love for them and Israel. Frankly, there have been occasions when, explaining why I as a Gentile Christian care about Jewish people and Israel, I have felt a bit like my old EL AL seatmate. For sometimes it is very hard to be a Christian who loves Jews.

Let me explain.

I said earlier in this book that my plea is for an understanding between Jewish people and their evangelical friends. The air of suspicion and mistrust that has prevailed in the past must be put aside if we are to establish relationships that are in the best interests of Jews and Christians alike.

A basic area of misunderstanding by many Jewish people is the agenda that evangelicals are pursuing when approaching Jews in an attempt to establish a friendly relationship. A prevailing attitude seems to be "I wonder what this guy wants?" It becomes particularly tenuous if, somewhere along the line, the Christian happens to mention Jesus. As we well know, the majority of Jewish people have been programmed by history, contemporary culture, or direct warnings from assorted instructors that the mention of His name must be associated with devious intentions.

This has become such a problem that some elements in evangelical circles have ceased to use the English *Jesus* in favor of the transliterated *Yeshua*. While I have no problem with brethren who, out of sensitivity for Jewish friends, prefer Yeshua, I frankly wonder how many Jews react inwardly to the practice. For example, do most liberal American Jews, who are hardly well-versed in such terminology, understand what is going on? If they do, do they recognize that Yeshua and Jesus are one and the same Person and react negatively?

Indeed, many evangelical groups have become so intimidated by anticipated negative reactions from Jewish individuals and agencies that they send up-front messages proclaiming that they will not evangelize Jews. I found it quite ironic to have read a statement some years ago by an evangelical group operating in Israel to the effect that "as an organization, we are thoroughly committed to evangelicals; however, we do not evangelize Jews."

To be honest, this is an astonishing contradiction in terms. It is true, of course, that sane and sensible evangelicals do not see every association and event as an evangelistic mission, nor do we fly in the face of national laws or public propriety. However, every true evangelical is called to be unequivocally committed to the mandate to make Christ known. Whatever else can be said, the very nature of evangelical Christianity is to evangelize. Sadly, the fundamental nature of what it means to evangelize is a matter that has escaped many Jewish people for centuries.

Nowhere is this better illustrated than in Israel's so-called "Anti-Missionary Law." Here is its text.

ENTICEMENT TO CHANGE OF RELIGION

Giving of "Bonuses" As Enticement to a Change of Religion:

He who gives, or promises to give money, an equivalent (of money), or whatever other benefit in order to entice a person to change his religion or in order to entice a person to bring about a change of another's religion, the sentence due to him is that of five years imprisonment, or a fine of IL 50,000.

Receiving of "Bonuses" in Exchange for a Change of Religion:

He who receives, or agrees to receive money, an equivalent (of money), or a benefit in exchange for a promise to change his religion, or to bring about a change in another's religion, the sentence due to him is that of three years imprisonment, or a fine of IL 30,000.[15]

To every reputable evangelical Christian I know, of whatever stripe, this legislation can only be described as preposterous. The thought of buying or inducing anyone to convert to Christianity is a blatant contradiction of everything Christianity stands for; evangelical Christians are not in the business of buying souls.

To Make Him Known

The commission given to Christians in the area of evangelism is actually very simple: Christians are commanded to make Christ known.

Immediately before His ascension to heaven from Jerusalem's Mount of Olives, Jesus gave specific instructions to His disciples: "Ye shall be witnesses unto me both in Jerusalem and in all Judea and in Samaria and unto the uttermost part of the earth" (Acts 1:8). The commission is further clarified in Romans 1:16, where we find that the gospel was to be presented "to the Jew first, and also to the Greek."

It is a matter of simple historic fact that the vast majority of the early recipients of the gospel were Jews. This was so much the case that when the numerical balance swung toward the church being populated more by Gentiles than by Jews, a warning was issued. Gentile believers were reminded that they were grafted in by God's grace and mercy, contrary to what they deserved (see Romans 11). Therefore Gentiles were admonished never to feel in any way superior to Jewish people who did not share their faith.

Why?

Because of God's love and larger purposes for the Jewish people.

"As concerning the gospel, they are enemies for your sakes, but as touching the election, they are beloved for the fathers' sakes. For the gifts and calling of God are without repentance" (Romans 11:28,29).

In other words, God has not changed His mind about what He promised to Abraham and his posterity. One day every promise made to Jewry will be lived out on the stage of human history in the minutest detail. In the interim, Christian believers have an obligation to honor His Word and His Chosen People. The very nature of the Christian lifestyle and attitude toward the sons and daughters of Abraham is to depict what it means to have been "grafted in" to God's favor by His grace through faith in Christ.

The message that Gentile believers are charged to make known is the simple word of God's grace and peace through Jesus Christ. This is the same message first brought to Gentiles by the first-century Jewish believers in

Jesus—those who had received Him as the Messiah of Israel and the Savior of the Gentiles who would likewise believe.

The message itself—the gospel—is encapsulated in 1 Corinthians 15:3,4: "For I delivered unto you first of all that which I also received, that Christ died for our sins according to the Scriptures, and that he was buried, and that he rose again the third day according to the Scriptures."

"According to the Scriptures" encompasses the entirety of the messianic prophecies found in the Old Testament and fulfilled in Jesus of Nazareth. In the Gospels, therefore, Jesus is presented as the Redeemer and sufficient Savior for all who believe, both Jews and Gentiles. This is the message that evangelicals make known.

However, to make Him known can never be equated with forcing people to believe the Christian message. To imply that evangelicals who share their faith with sensitivity and integrity are on a crusade to destroy Judaism and mutilate Jewry is a serious breach of fairness.

Are Evangelicals Seeking to Destroy Judaism?

I was asked this question recently by a reporter seeking, I later learned, to find the worst things he could print about Christians like myself.

"Well," I replied, "if it hasn't been done in 2000 years, I think you have little to worry about from this generation of Christians."

I went on to make the point that the primary challenge to Judaism today does not come from evangelical Christians but rather from assimilation—an observation agreed to by some eminent Jewish thinkers.

Rabbi Daniel Lapin, founder of the conservative group Toward Tradition, writes:

At speeches to Jewish audiences all around the country I am often asked for my reaction to the threat posed to the Jewish community by Christian missionary activity. I know that this matter is of enormous concern to many Jews. My answer is that we are indeed losing vast numbers of Jews—but chiefly to assimilation and secularism. Those few that do convert to Christianity are not yeshiva graduates. Instead they are bewildered Jews who often sought spiritual guidance from their local temples and rabbis but sought in vain. What they were offered in place of the transcendent values they wanted was typical liberal activism.[16]

The reporter then asked a related question, which, to my way of thinking, was much more lucid: "Do you feel that Jews can find a sense of personal fulfillment in Judaism?"

My answer was, "Of course they can, and thousands do."

As a matter of fact, numbers of formerly secular Jews in Israel are turning to Orthodox Judaism in their search for spiritual fulfillment.

"Why then," he wondered, "are so many Jews listening to Christians, cultists, or New Agers?"

"I suspect," I responded, "for the same reasons many nominal Christians are listening to cultists and New Agers: the failure of liberal religion."

There are significant similarities between developments in Judaism and in mainline denominational Christianity, in that both have failed the people they are charged to nurture and shepherd. Liberal Judaism and liberal Christianity have become bodies without a soul. When people turn from the precepts and practices of Scripture in favor of cultural forms and traditional loyalties void of the absolutes established by God, you can rest assured that the flock, whether Jewish or Christian, will not stay in the fold.

Both liberal Jews and liberal Christians can cry wolf as loudly as they like and blame a variety of "competitors" for their own failures, but the fact remains that "Where there is no vision [revelation from God], the people perish" (Proverbs 29:18). In other words, *Go somewhere else to look for light.*

Are Evangelicals Attempting to Mutilate Jewry?

This is an accusation that is extremely difficult for evangelicals to fathom. It is, after all, evangelical Christians who accept as historical and irrevocable God's promises to Abraham and his physical posterity. This being true, it follows that they would be the last people on earth to contribute to the diminishing of the Jewish people.

Thus Christians cringe and reasonable Jewish people turn red with embarrassment when statements are made such as those by Mark Powers of Jews for Judaism, asserting "that [for Jews] to forge relationships with groups who are dedicated to converting Jews is like cooperation with the Nazis. Both have the same goal—the end of the Jewish people" (*The Jewish Exponent*, April 28, 1995).

One Jewish voice of reason is that of Herbert Zweibon, head of Americans for a Safe Israel. Zweibon, who is not offended by evangelicals making their message known to Jews, says, "Like Jews, like any other religion, they are entitled to present their perspective as 'the right way'" (*The Detroit Jewish News*, July 28, 1995).

Powers' inflammatory accusation represents an attitude that could not be more counterproductive for the Jewish people. I know of no evangelical in my theological circle who would ever accuse a Jewish person, including

Mr. Powers or any member of his group, of being a "Christ killer." That appellation, I suspect, is probably only slightly more abhorrent to Jews as is being associated with Adolf Hitler to honorable Christians.

It is a matter of record that many evangelicals, like myself, devote a considerable amount of time and energy speaking and writing against the demonic "Christ killer" folly and defending the moral integrity of the Jewish people.

But of far greater consequence is the implication leveled at evangelical Christians, who are without question the most dedicated allies that Israel and the Jewish people have on earth. As is commonly known, they number in the millions, and to recklessly attack such a support base is a very serious tactical, as well as moral, error.

Evangelicals have a difficult time comprehending the concept that when a Jew becomes a believer in Jesus, he is no longer considered a Jew. He was born of a Jewish mother and therefore has an acceptable amount of Jewish blood coursing through his veins.

Concerning matters of religious persuasion, a Jew can be an agnostic, an atheist, or a follower of a self-proclaimed messiah, such as the late Rabbi Schneerson, and still be accepted as a Jew and welcomed in the community. But to become a believer in Jesus is quite another issue and is, as I have said, perplexing to Christians.

I, for example, am of Scotch-Irish-German descent. Not having been reared as a Christian or identified with a church or particular denomination, this labeled me, I suppose, as a civilized pagan. When I became a Christian, my lifestyle took a radical turn, to say the least. As a Christian I was most certainly out of sync with the religious and moral views of many of my relatives. I was, however, no less Scotch-Irish-German; the bloodline remains the same. While I am fully aware of the declarations of non-Jewishness assigned to Jews who become believers in Jesus, the question remains: Why is a Jew who believes in Jesus less a Jew than one who believes in no God at all?

Jews in the Pew

As for those Jewish people who are written off by their own brethren because they have become believers in Jesus, there is this to say: A Jew in a church is an extremely good investment for the Jewish community and the State of Israel. This may sound absurd to many Jews, particularly those who are practicing their faith, but I assure you it is true.

For the past 20 years I have been lecturing about the Jewish people, Israel, and biblical prophecy in Christian churches of various denominations. Virtually without exception, where Jewish people are in attendance, the entire complexion of the congregation has changed.

Because of a Jewish presence, pastors are more concerned about biblical associations with Christianity's Old Testament roots and are more inclined to speak on related themes. Congregants are much more sensitive to their relationship to the Jewish community, as well as to their Jewish brother and sister in the faith. In short, while the Jewish community at large may see a fellow Jew in a church as a loss, I can tell you that a single Jew among Christians is worth more to Jewry than a thousand position papers on Israel and anti-Semitism.

From another perspective—and I say this with all due respect—that scorned and rejected son or daughter of Abraham in a church pew is of far more practical value to world Jewry than a fully embraced Jewish atheist sunning himself on the beach at Tel Aviv.

Thank God for Israel Days

There is a growing desire among evangelical churches to establish constructive relationships with the members of the Jewish community. Therefore more and more churches are setting aside specific days on which to invite members of the Jewish community to attend a service dedicated to expressing appreciation for the Jewish people and solidarity with Israel. These programs, if properly done, can bridge significant barriers between Jewish people and their Christian neighbors.

While these special days are becoming popular across the country, I cite one example from a church in Florida. The Boca Raton Bible Church scheduled a Thank God for Israel Day and went all out to make the occasion something very special for the church and their Jewish guests. Invitations went out to leaders of Jewish religious, social, and political groups. The response was overwhelming: Approximately 2000 people, with a large contingent from various sectors of the Jewish community, filled the auditorium on the Sunday morning in February designated as Thank God for Israel Day at Boca Raton Bible Church.

The auditorium was beautifully decorated, themed toward Israel, and decked with the blue–and–white national emblems of the State. The music and special presentations were all geared toward appreciation for the contributions that Jewry had made in providing the roots for our Christian faith. The sermon was built around biblical associations and mandates for solidarity with Israel and the need to stand together on matters of mutual concern in confronting challenges to our Judeo-Christian heritage.

At the conclusion of the service, a reception was held in honor of the Jewish guests of the congregation.

The net result was that members of the Boca Raton Bible Church left as boosters of Israel, dedicated to establishing or renewing ties in the Jewish community. Jewish people came away with a new degree of understanding and appreciation for these firm friends of Israel and the

Jewish people who were willing to put their friendship on the public record. In the process, the anti-Semites in the area got the message that this was a church ready to stand up and be counted when it came to the question of where Jews could find their friends.

These are firmly committed evangelical Christians, by all means, but also Christians with integrity and a sensitivity toward their Jewish neighbors that reflected the true spirit of the Christ they serve and the brand of Christianity they embody.

In the Arena

The evangelicals' desire to make Christ known moves objectively in widening circles. Certainly they wish to bring the message of the Messiah to the Jewish people. But of no less importance is taking the gospel to all of humanity—beginning with people in their most immediate sphere of influence, and then to those beyond. In other words, evangelicals see the first need for the gospel in their own personal lives and the lives of their families, and then a responsibility to bear a credible witness before others.

To be a witness of the Christian faith involves many elements, but for all truly credible Christians, the watchword of witness is *integrity*. It is an integrity not simply driven by what we might term *good sales procedures*. Indeed, true evangelical believers communicate the gospel out of a sense of obedience to the commission given to them by Christ. Such obedience, however, is coupled with a genuine sense of appreciation for what they personally have experienced through faith in Him.

Jesus Christ—who lived as a Jew among the Jewish people, preached and taught from the Hebrew Scriptures, ascended from the Mount of Olives in Jerusalem, and promised to return to that city and reconciled Israel—has revolutionized the lives and altered the destiny of evangelical believers. Therefore it seems but a natural consequence of such a relationship that believers possess an affinity for Jewish people and a sense of debt or gratitude to the people who were guardians of the Scriptures and through whom Jesus came to us.

Evangelicals are not scalp-hunting marauders or entrenched enemies of the Jewish people. Those who portray them as such are creating an erroneous image.

Do evangelicals desire to make Christ known to their Jewish friends? Indeed they do, but with respect and integrity. They are always sensitive to the fact that their responsibility is limited to *making Him known*. What their hearers do with that information must be between those individuals and God. Their decision must be just that—their own decision.

It cannot be stressed strongly enough: *Evangelical Christians seek only the opportunity to be heard*. Whether Jews or Gentiles wish to listen is their choice—one that will be respected. What they choose to do is, I say again, theirs to decide.

To summarize, here are the ground rules that responsible evangelicals scrupulously observe.

- Our commitment to Jesus Christ compels us to make Him known, through the message of the gospel, to all people. The church has been so commissioned.
- Coercion through deception, inducement, or emotional manipulation is abhorrent and contrary to the message and spirit of Christ and the gospel.
- People who become believers in Christ must do so of their own free will and with a clear understanding of the implications of their decision.
- Propagators of the Christian faith act with a level of integrity consistent with standards acceptable in any arena where the free exchange of ideas is encouraged, and are not to be viewed as people to fear.

103

I have been puzzled for years by a perplexing question: Why is it that the majority of Jewish people, often those most skilled in public discourse and debate, seem totally intimidated by the thought of entering a conversation about Christ and Christianity? I am thoroughly familiar with the distasteful memories carried by Jewry from the Holocaust and persecutions leveled against Jews by pseudo-Christians in days gone by. However, considering the realities of this generation, and the positive way evangelicals have related to Jewish people in America, a Jewish person should feel no more intimidated at hearing a Christian make a case for his faith than does an evangelical at hearing a Jew make the case for Judaism.

In my own experience, I can say that when engaged in dialogue with Jewish people about matters of faith, I have never had what I would consider an unpleasant experience. Did I convince every Jewish person with whom I had a conversation to become a believer in Jesus? By no means. But we talked, they decided, and—to the person, I felt—they left with a sense of friendship and better understanding of what the Christian faith is all about.

But this is a new day and a time when some large issues of grave mutual concern confront both communities. We believe it is time for American Jews to learn just what evangelical Christians are all about, and a time for evangelical Christians to get to know the Jewish community and their concerns.

I have always been intrigued by how Christians respond to the Jewish people and Israel when given the right information. As I mentioned previously, for more than two decades I have traveled throughout America and in numerous other countries speaking on Israel and the Middle East, Bible prophecy, the rights of Jews in the land, the miracle of modern Israel, the plague of Islamic terror, and like subjects. Invariably I encounter an outpouring of love, support, and solidarity for Israel and the Jewish people that is thrilling to witness.

It doesn't seem to matter whether I am in an auditorium addressing 50 people or 5000—there is always an element of enthusiastic response from earnest people seeking ways to show their love and support for the nation and its people, and declaring their determination to "pray for the peace of Jerusalem."

Oddly enough, many of these Christians are not personally acquainted with a Jewish person, nor have they ever been to Israel. But there is something within them prompting genuine and unconditional love for the Jewish people. I suppose it could be called a simple, God-given matter of the heart.

I consistently experience the same manifestation among people we have taken to Israel—many thousands over the years. I can probably count on the fingers of one hand those who were unimpressed and had no desire to return. To see them mingling with Israelis, standing in awe at the biblical and historical sights, watching their expressions as they thrust hands into the soil to place memorial trees in the ground, and listening to them sobbing at Yad Vashem are quite remarkable experiences. Unquestionably, there is a magnetism about Israel and its people that cannot be explained in casual terms or compared to any other experience that a Christian can observe.

I have often wished that every Jewish person alive today, particularly those who question the motives of evangelical Christians, could stand with me at such times. They would see, as I do, that these are people who just love Jews and Israel. They have no axes to grind, no quest for souls to subvert, no desire to force any unwanted decision, no exploitive agendas to pursue. On the contrary, the overwhelming majority of evangelical Christians leave the land of Israel as better informed people who are boosters of the nation and true friends of the Jewish people.

Do you remember the California businessman I met on the EL AL flight to Israel? He was the man who had been reared in Canada, and was chased home from school by young toughs calling him a "Christ killer." You will remember that, thinking they were all Christians, he grew up hating them and everything they stood for. Upon learning that I was a Christian with a love for Israel and Jewish people, he asked me to sit with him for a time.

"You know," he said, "even though I hated them so intensely, I have hoped, in spite of it, that somewhere, sometime, I would meet someone who could tell me about Jesus Christ and know what he was talking about. I think I've found that man today. Will you tell me about Jesus Christ?"

I did. After an extended conversation, in which I tried my best to answer his questions, he took my hand in both of his.

"I want to tell you something," he said with a smile. "First, I want you to know that you didn't make a Christian out of me today. But I also want to tell you that you have given me a lot to think about."

I haven't seen or heard from him since, but I feel that our encounter represents what I am trying to say. Jewish people need not fear listening to followers of Jesus, who will in most cases be speaking out of a sincere and honest heart. Christians cannot decide anything for Jews, and will not attempt to do so. So what's to fear?

6

The Returns Converge

The State of Israel has risen.
—David Ben Gurion, May 14, 1948

The return of evangelical commitment to giving Israel her proper place in future events ran roughly parallel to the rising desire of Jewish people to return to the land of their fathers. The phenomenon takes on immense significance when we look at what was developing simultaneously within the Zionist movement and in the evangelical community. Such stirrings were not recognized as a formal alliance by either group at the time. In hindsight, however, they seem to have been pushed in the same direction by a higher hand.

For Jews, the terrible pogroms that took place in Czarist Russia in 1881 were forcing the issue of where Jews could find a safe haven. Of course, the enduring

dream of scattered Jewry had always been "the Hope"—
a return to Zion. For nearly 2000 years, "next year in
Jerusalem" had been the final word around Jewish
Passover tables the world over.

That hope is memorialized today each time Israelis
rise to sing their national anthem, "Hatikva."

> So long as still within our breasts
> The Jewish heart beats true,
> So long as still towards the east
> To Zion looks the Jew,
> So long our hopes are not yet lost—
> Two thousand years we cherished them—
> To live in freedom in the land
> Of Zion and Jerusalem.

Events crescendoed to a climax of sorts with the 1894
trial of Alfred Dreyfus in Paris. Dreyfus, the only Jewish
member of the general staff of the French army, was
accused of treason. After two trials and wearying years in
prison, the officer was exonerated of all charges against
him. However, the anti-Semitic fervor fanned by the trial
left European Jewry in shock.

Among the stunned observers was a Jewish journalist,
Theodor Herzl, who had for some time had doubts about
the quality of European hospitality toward the Jew. Those
doubts were confirmed by the Dreyfus affair, and Herzl
became convinced that it was time for European Jews to
prepare to make a move. Herzl, revered as the father of
modern Zionism and founder of the Jewish State, began
to promote the dream of a return of Jews to their ancient
homeland in Palestine. The tone of his urgings was sum-
marized in a simple phrase: "If you will it," said Herzl, "it
is no dream."

On August 31, 1897, at Basel, Switzerland, Herzl
convened the First Zionist Congress. When it ended,

Herzl wrote in his diary, "At Basle I founded the Jewish state." Although the realization of Herzl's dream was still some years away, a page had been turned in Jewish history, and a new reality entered the world of the Jew.

In the Christian world, on both sides of the Atlantic, a similar tide was rising among those biblically committed to a Jewish return.

Jesus Is Coming

An American milestone was reached with the 1878 publication of William E. Blackstone's book *Jesus Is Coming*. The book instantly became a phenomenal success, and sales were soon being counted in the hundreds of thousands. The work, which is read as a classic today, has sold well over a million copies and has been translated into 47 languages.

Jewish author Michael Pragai, in his book *Faith and Fulfillment*, sized up Blackstone with the following words:

> The author was a Chicago businessman, William E. Blackstone, a stout Christian Evangelist missionary and an ardent supporter of a Jewish revival in Zion. Blackstone was an outstanding Biblical scholar, and his "Zionist" views sprang from his Millenary theology. In his book, which came out in many translations, including Hebrew, he saw the Jewish Res- toration of Zion as the fulfillment of the Biblical prophecies heralding the approach of the Second Advent of Christ.
>
> Like other Christian theologians, he raised the question of how Israel's survival over generations is to be interpreted. And Blackstone answered:
>
> "And the wonderful preservation, as a distinct people, through all the persecutions,

vicissitudes and wanderings of the past eighteen centuries down to this present moment, is a standing miracle, attesting to the truth of God's word, and assuring His purposes in their future history.

"Said Frederick the Great to his chaplain: 'Doctor, if your religion is a true one, it ought to be capable of a very brief and simple truth. Will you give me an evidence of its truth in one word?' The good man answered—'Israel.'

"Other nations come and go, but Israel remains. She passes not away.

"God says of her: 'For a small moment have I forsaken thee, but with great mercies will I gather thee. In a little wrath I hid my face from thee for a moment, but with everlasting kindness will I have mercy on thee, saith the LORD, thy Redeemer' (Isaiah 54:7,8)."[17]

Blackstone's belief, "Happy is the people that shall intercede on Israel's behalf, for God hath said: 'I will bless them that bless thee,' " was something he practiced literally. President Woodrow Wilson was favorably influenced through Blackstone's intercession to support the Balfour Declaration, which called for a homeland for Jews in Palestine.

As with other premillennial thinkers, Blackstone believed firmly that the Jewish people had never relinquished their rights to the land given by God to Abraham. He said:

> The Jews have never abandoned this land of their own will, and they have not signed any treaty of capitulation, but they have succumbed in a desperate battle before the crushing power of Rome....They were sold as

slaves....The violence by which Israel was kept out of her land, without means of appeal, is in principle equivalent to a continual conflict....No entreaty can change this situation until Israel will have the opportunity to present its demands before the one and only competent Authority, an international Conference.[18]

Other Supporters

From another Jewish source, *The Encyclopedia of Zionism and Israel,* we find an assessment of other evangelicals who were supportive of a Jewish return.

It should be noted that the idea of a Jewish return to Palestine had long found strong support among prominent Christians in Western Europe, particularly in England. Eminent men and women lent themselves to what came to be known as the Restoration Movement, which favored the ingathering of Jews to their Homeland on the ground of Christian doctrine.... It is difficult to say to what extent such pro-Zionist sentiments among Christian leaders influenced the Jews, but in all likelihood they helped pave the way for British acceptance of Zionism later on.[19]

As early as the 1840s, some influential Christians were telling their peers that they should be encouraging the concept of a Jewish return. There were many who held this conviction and who to a greater or lesser degree played active roles in the movement. Among the better-known was the great social reformer Lord Shaftsbury. Pragai notes:

He fought for the idea of the Return just as much as for his many other social or philanthropic undertakings. But in the case of the Jews there were many additional dimensions: attachment to the Bible and the opportunity of helping biblical prophecy to its fulfillment. Lord Shaftsbury, like many other stout Protestants, held the belief of the Second Advent. And since, according to prophecy, the Return of the Jews is indispensable to this great event, [he] never doubted that the Jews were to return to their own land. This was his daily prayer, his daily hope. "Oh, pray for the peace of Jerusalem" were the words engraved on the ring he always wore on his right hand.[20]

Lawrence Oliphant was also among those in the British Restoration Movement who favored a Jewish return to Palestine. Oliphant, an officer in the British Foreign Service, served in the Parliament in the late 1860s. Deeply moved by the anti-Semitic outbursts he witnessed in Romania, he proceeded to survey lands east of the Jordan—ancient Gilead—as a place to resettle Jews from Europe. Oliphant took his plan to the Sultan in Constantinople and the Turkish cabinet, both of whom approved of designating a million-and-a-half acres for Jewish settlement. The plan was scuttled, however, by Sultan Abdul Hamid, who suspected British political intrigue.

Oliphant's Christian passion, which he urged from a "Biblical point of view," never wavered. Following the massive pogroms against Jewish communities in Russia in 1881, he gathered a group of influential Christians in London to promote the idea of building Jewish villages in Gilead. Furthermore, Oliphant advised Jewish organizations, who sought to save Jews in Russia by aiding their immigration to the United States, to encourage them instead to go to Palestine.

So strong and obvious to the Jewish people was Oliphant's desire to aid in a Jewish return that Israel has honored his memory by naming a street in Jerusalem after him.

Herzl and Hechler

Theodor Herzl had his dream, but he clearly needed influential people who shared it. Yes, there were other Jews, visionaries, who saw the future as he did. But, strange as it may seem now that we are on the other side of the Holocaust, he had stern opposition from unlikely sources. Among Herzl's own friends were those who confided that he had gone quite mad. Some went so far as to counsel him to see a psychiatrist. Frontal opposition came from prominent rabbinical forces in Germany, who officially advised Jews to shun Zionism.

There were others, however, who thought Herzl was right on the mark and a person who, like Esther of old, was called into the arena "for such a time as this" (Esther 4:14). Among them was the venerable British clergyman William H. Hechler. When Herzl and Hechler first met, on March 10, 1896, they seemed like an odd pairing. Herzl was the picture of a dignified Jewish journalist. Hechler, on the other hand, was an unconventional Christian who was, in Herzl's words, "curious and complicated…given to pedantry, undue humility, and much pious rolling of the eyes" (*Prince and Prophet*, p. 43).

Hechler, however, was a man with an enormous circle of contacts that ran through the ranks of Protestant officials and into the courts of European royalty. Yes, Herzl needed contacts badly, and in Hechler he had found the right man.

When all was said and done, Herzl would declare of the man who became a trusted and valued friend, "He

113

counsels me superbly, and with unmistakably genuine good will. He is at once shrewd and mystical, cunning and naive. So far, with respect to myself, he has backed me up in quite a wonderful way....I would wish the Jews to show him a full measure of gratitude" (*Prince and Prophet*, p. 43).

The British clergyman's enthusiasm for what he saw in Herzl and the Zionists he was coming in contact with made it hard for him to conceal his enthusiasm.

> We are now seeing the stirrings of the bones in Ezekiel's valley: O! may we soon see the glorious outpourings of the spiritual life predicted in Ezekiel 36. The religious element is, according to God's word, to become the inspiring force, and, I think, I can see that it is the religious faith in Zionism, which is now influencing the whole nation of the Jews... what food for reflection to every thoughtful student of the Bible and history.
>
> The Jews are beginning to look forward to and believe in the glorious future of their nation, when, instead of being a curse, they are once more to become a blessing to all.[21]

The quality of their relationship is reflected in a letter that Hechler wrote to Herzl from Vienna when the latter was perplexed over being rebuffed by some important members of European royalty.

> I am very worried on your account. I am afraid that in your impulsiveness you will only succeed in hitting your head against the wall. Let me ask you not to rush too much. The great ones of the world have to be tamed. If all this [the Jewish return to Palestine] seems

impossible to thousands of the children of Abraham, and not so desirable, how much more impossible will it seem to those [Gentiles] who know nothing about the matter? Please be very discreet concerning the subject of which you write and the manner in which you do it. For the good of your cause, I pray that you will let me see what you write before sending it, being one who can judge impartially from the side.[22]

But for all their camaraderie, there was still the lurking suspicion that Jewish people, in the best of relationships with caring Christians, find hard to shake. After Hechler issued an invitation to Herzl to attend an Anglican service at which he was preaching and the British ambassador would be reading Scripture, Herzl made a revealing observation. Hechler wrote to his friend:

It is nearly midnight, and my thoughts are flying toward Jerusalem and the Holy Land.... What can be done to awaken those sleeping lazy Christians? On Sunday morning I will preach about the return of the Jews to Palestine....Do come, Dr. Herzl. Come Sunday morning at 11 o'clock. The sermon is given at ten minutes to twelve, but one should be there at eleven in order to hear His Excellency officiate. This is good advice.... May God guide and bless us![23]

In his journal on the same day, after commenting on the exceptional devotion of Hechler, Herzl added, "But I think he wants to convert me."

Certainly Hechler would have liked to restore the

messianic aspiration to his friend Herzl. But on that particular occasion he wished only for Herzl's presence to make a favorable impression on the ambassador, Sir Monson, and thus promote the cause so dear to them both.

Herzl's passing was a traumatic event for Hechler. He spoke for many Jews when, after Herzl's funeral in Vienna, he said, "But this evening they [Jews] will be clear of the streets of this anti-Semitic city, taking their trains back to their reserved neighborhoods....Only now they ask with tears of despair: Who will lead us now to the promised, inaccessible land?"

For many years after his friend's death, Hechler continued to champion, among sluggish Christians the return of the Jews to Zion. And he was not alone; there were others who stood ready to make the dream a reality.

Philipp Newlinski

Another of Herzl's Christian counselors, Philipp Newlinski, was also an ardent supporter of the biblical concept of a Jewish return. While Hechler's contacts had been for the most part in England and the royal courts of Europe, Newlinski's took Herzl in another direction. As a journalist appointed to the Austro-Hungarian Embassy in Constantinople, he knew the situation in Turkey and the Near East well. It was a time when the Muslim Ottoman Turks were ruling Palestine from Constantinople.

On Herzl's behalf, Newlinski contacted the Turkish Sultan, the Crown Prince of Bulgaria, the German Chancellor, and the Vatican. While not successful in every attempt, he relentlessly promoted the return of Jews to Palestine, with the net effect of making the movement well-known in many royal courts.

The Balfour Declaration

In December 1917, General Edmund Allenby led the British Expeditionary Force in a World War I campaign that routed Turkish forces from Palestine and captured the City of Jerusalem. Allenby and the allied Western forces would occupy the largest area in the Middle East ever conquered by "Christian" nations.

One of the most moving demonstrations of Christian reverence for the city so loved by Jews was displayed by the conquering commander of the British Expeditionary Force. General Allenby rode at the head of a long procession toward the Old City on his way to officially accept the surrender of Jerusalem from the Turks. Upon arriving at the Jaffa Gate, the general suddenly reined in his horse and dismounted. When asked why he was doing such a thing, he replied: "Because it is not fitting that I should ride mounted across the stones where my Lord carried His cross."

Even before Allenby's famous entry into Jerusalem, however, the British government had declared itself in favor of a homeland for Jews in Palestine.

On November 2, 1917, the British took a major step toward the rebirth of the modern State of Israel. It came in a letter from the British Foreign Secretary, Lord Arthur James Balfour, to the renowned Jewish leader Lord Rothschild. The text of the declaration read:

> Dear Lord Rothschild,
>
> I have the pleasure in conveying to you, on behalf of His Majesty's Government, the following declaration of sympathy with the Jewish Zionist aspirations which have been submitted to, and approved by, the Cabinet.
>
> His Majesty's Government views with favor the establishment in Palestine of a national

home for the Jewish people, and will use our best endeavors to facilitate the achievement of this object, it being clearly understood that nothing shall be done which may prejudice the civil and religious rights of existing non-Jewish communities in Palestine, or the rights and political status enjoyed by Jews in any other country.

I should be grateful if you would bring this declaration to the knowledge of the Zionist Federation.

Yours sincerely,
Arthur James Balfour

As was true with the development of early Zionism, the road to the Balfour Declaration was paved with relationships between Jews and those special types of Christians who believed that they should help make a way home for the Jewish people.

John Henry Patterson

As World War I was progressing, men like Lieutenant Colonel John Henry Patterson were putting feet to their biblical convictions. Patterson was a devout Christian who was brought up under strict biblical discipline, which included intense Bible study. Bible geography, prophecies about Israel, and a thorough familiarity with the great stories of the Book stood him in good stead when he was appointed to command the Zion Mule Corps. He also became a strong advocate for the formation of a Jewish Legion to fight with the British against the Turks. When Patterson, the Christian, was appointed to lead the newly formed Jewish fighting force, he became the commander of the first Jewish fighting brigade to campaign in the Holy Land since the Bar Kokhba rebellion against the

Romans in 135 A.D. Patterson related his feelings as a Christian about the Balfour Declaration.

> Christians, too, have always believed in the fulfillment of prophecy, and the Restoration of the Jewish people is of no little interest to them, so it can be imagined with what feelings of joy and gratitude the masses of the Jewish people looked upon the promise of England, holding out as it did the prospect of the realization of their dearest hope. Nothing like it has been known since the days of King Cyrus. It is not too much to say that this epoch-making Declaration uplifted the soul of Israel the world over.[24]

Wyndham Deedes

Sir Wyndham Deedes was known for "the humble simplicity of his faith [which] was at one with the humble simplicity of his nature. He spent much time in contemplation, especially in the early hours of the morning, and a Bible was always at his bedside."

During World War I, Deedes was stationed in Cairo, serving in the British Intelligence Service. It was there that he met Dr. Chaim Weizman, a Jewish champion of Zionism who would later become Israel's first President. It was Deedes who informed a rather surprised Weizman of the taint of anti-Semitism infecting the British military—a fact that was to become a decided problem for Jews during the pre-state days of the British Mandate.

At their first meeting in the tent of General Allenby, Deedes pulled out a typed copy of the so-called *Protocols of the Elders of Zion*.

Weizman asked him what "this rubbish" was.

Deedes told the baffled Jew, "You will find it in the

haversack of a great many British officers here—and they believe it!"

The British intelligence officer went on to explain that copies of the *Protocols* had been brought over by the British military mission that had been serving on the staff of Grand Duke Nicholas in the Russian Caucasus.

Exposing the *Protocols* to Weizman would greatly enhance his perspective in future dealings with certain elements in the British military.

Like the others who were Christian lovers of the land and its people, Wyndham Deedes' fervor was nurtured by deep biblical roots. Professor Norman Bentwich, an associate in the early Palestine Administration, wrote of him:

> He was a deeply religious Christian and conscious of the inhumanity which the professed Christian states of Europe had shown to the Jews for centuries. He was convinced that the Christian society should make retribution for that age-long injustice, and assist the Jews to establish their National Home in the Bible Land.[25]

Balfour and Lloyd George

Two key players in the British government at the time of the Balfour Declaration were Prime Minister David Lloyd George and British Foreign Secretary Lord Arthur James Balfour.

Balfour, who would lend his name to the famous Declaration, was steeped in the Old Testament from his childhood. Historian Michael Pragai said of him:

> He was one of those devout Christians who was able to view the Jews with insight and simple, down-to-earth understanding. For

Balfour the Jews were not the instruments of a Christian Millennium or, as others had suggested, tools of development projects in the neglected Ottoman Near East. They were, rather, exiles who needed help to get back to their homeland. Why there? "The answer is," he wrote, "that the position of the Jew is unique. For them race, religion and country are inter-related as they are inter-related in the case of no other religion and no other country on earth."[26]

For a man the likes of Arthur Balfour, the Declaration bearing his name was simply the honorable and biblical thing to do.

David Lloyd George, England's Prime Minister from 1916 to 1922, was no less a biblicist when it came to the matter of a Jewish return to Palestine. He remembered his youth as a time when "I was taught far more about the history of the Jews than about the history of my own people."

When speaking about the Balfour Declaration, Lloyd George was emphatic: "It was undoubtedly inspired by natural sympathy, admiration and also by the fact that, as you must remember, we had been trained even more in Hebrew history than in the history of our own country. I could tell you all the kings of Israel. But I doubt whether I could have named half a dozen of the kings of England!"

Lloyd George felt a deep debt of gratitude to Chaim Weizman, a biochemist who had invented a chemical process which the British urgently needed during the war. This no doubt weighed heavily upon his and the War Department's decision regarding the Balfour Declaration. But, in the minds of many, this was a subsidiary consideration to what their biblical backgrounds were prompting them to do.

In fact, it was Lloyd George who insisted that the original borders of the proposed Jewish homeland approximate those laid out in the Abrahamic Covenant.

Speaking of these men and their storied Declaration, Lieutenant Colonel Patterson wrote:

> Britain's share towards the fulfillment of prophecy must...not be forgotten and the names of Mr. Lloyd George and Sir Arthur Balfour, two men raised up to deal justly with Israel, will, I feel sure, live for all time in the hearts and affections of the Jewish people. It is owing to the stimulus given by the Balfour Declaration to the soul of Jewry throughout the world that we are now looking upon the wonderful spectacle unfolding before our eyes, of the people returning to the Land promised to Abraham and his seed forever.[27]

Blanche Dugdale

Among the host of dedicated Christian women who shared a biblical zeal for a Jewish national home was Blanche Dugdale. She was the niece of Lord Balfour and an outspoken advocate of Jewish rights in the Middle East.

Lady Dugdale knew and loved the Word of God. Consequently she had a great heart for the Jewish people and Israel. She was a particular favorite of Dr. Weizman, who spoke of her as "an ardent, lifelong friend of Zionism." For many years she promoted Zionism among British statesmen. In addition, she functioned as an adviser to the Zionist leadership during the years of the British Mandate.

Blanche Dugdale had the perception to see what was ahead for the Jews in Hitler's Europe. During World War II she worked tirelessly, constantly speaking in public meetings, attempting to secure help for children who had been victimized by the Nazis.

This good woman believed that there was no alternative for the Jewish people, who had been ravished in the trauma that was World War II, than to create a national safe haven in Israel. Her conviction was based on her unwavering belief that this was true because Israel was a land grant made by God to the Jewish people in perpetuity.

She died on May 15, 1948—the day the State of Israel became a reality.

Orde Wingate

Perhaps the best-known of all the true friends of Israel associated with the return to the Promised Land was a British army captain named Orde Wingate.

Wingate was not a person who moved in the higher echelons of government. He was rather an officer who, like Patterson, served in the field, working shoulder to shoulder with the Jewish defenders of life and land.

Wingate arrived in Palestine in 1936 while, under British Mandatory rule, Jewish returnees were attempting to maintain their still–fragile presence in their settlements. Unfortunately, they were not receiving overwhelming support from the British, who by this time had taken a turn toward the Arabs. Indeed, with all the foreboding developments in Europe, the British were moving toward a policy that would severely restrict Jewish immigration. The policy was deployed in 1939 through a series of "White Papers," which announced an absolute limit of 75,000 on Jewish immigration into Palestine.

It was during this time that Arabs were harassing Jewish settlers by, among other things, attacking buses, burning Jewish homes and fields, and carrying out sniping attacks on Jews traveling the roads or working in the fields. With the arrival of Orde Wingate, the Jews received a gift that would materially contribute to their ability to defend themselves. Of even greater importance was his aid in preparing them for the coming military struggle, when the very survival of the state was in question.

He entered Palestine with little knowledge of what was transpiring on the ground. He was well–versed in the arguments taking place among the British as to whether the Jews should have their own state or be kept a controlled minority living among the Arabs. These arguments, however, carried no weight with Wingate. He knew where his sympathies rested; he had learned it as a boy at the knee of his mother in far-off England.

His sister, Rachel, remembered that it was "mother who taught Orde about religion....She gave him a regular and systematic Bible training. She suckled him on the strong milk of the Old Testament and weaned him on the Psalms and Proverbs." Through her patient spiritual nurturing, Wingate became a lover of the Bible—so much so that it eventually shaped the whole course of his life.

Being in Israel, the place he already knew so much about, was an exhilarating experience for Wingate. Among his great delights was touring the land. He is well remembered for singing, in Hebrew, the 126th Psalm as he strode through the fields: "When the LORD turned again the captivity of Zion, we were like them that dream. Then was our mouth filled with laughter, and our tongue with singing; then said they among the nations, The LORD hath done great things for them. The LORD hath done great things for us, whereof we are glad."

When a prominent Jew from Haifa asked the captain about Zionism, Wingate replied, "I have met few Jews in my life, but my sympathies are with Zionism."

The man then asked him if he had read anything about Zionism.

Wingate was ready with his answer: "There is only one important book on the subject, the Bible, and I have read it thoroughly" (*Faith and Fulfillment*, p. 112).

It was Wingate who trained the Jewish settlers in the military art of disciplined self-defense. He developed the Special Night Squads, which soon struck fear into the Arab attack units that had been making night raids on Jewish kibbutzim. Arab guerrilla units crossing from Syria and Jordan soon found that they were being met by well-trained, professionally led opponents who were up to the task of thwarting their attempts to attack inadequately armed civilians.

To all those who trained and fought at his side—men like the famed Moshe Dyan—he became not only respected but revered as a leader. To his young Jewish comrades he became the *Yedid*, the friend. And that friendship has endured. To this day you can meet, as I have, many Jews who were trained by Orde Wingate. To the man, they speak of fond memories and unbridled appreciation for the young English soldier who was willing to give so much of himself for them and their land.

Of his part in their preparation, Wingate said:

> This is the cause of your survival. I count it as my privilege to help you fight your battle. To that purpose I want to devote my life. I believe that the very existence of mankind is justified when it is based on the moral foundation of the Bible. Whoever dares lift a hand against you and your enterprise here should be fought against. Whether it is jealousy, ignorance or perverted doctrine such as have made your neighbors rise against you, or politics which make some of my countrymen support them, I shall fight with you against any of

these influences. But remember that this is *your* battle. My part, which I say I feel to be a privilege, is only to help you.[28]

At a farewell party given in his honor, Orde Wingate let the Scriptures express his feelings: "If I forget thee, O Jerusalem, let my right hand forget her cunning. If I do not remember thee, let my tongue cleave to the roof of my mouth, if I prefer not Jerusalem above my chief joy" (Psalm 137:5,6).

A Jewish village, Yemin Orde, has been named in Wingate's honor. It could be viewed as tangible evidence of Jewish appreciation for him and the multitudes of evangelical Christians who have shared the single-hearted love for the land and the people of the Book exhibited by Orde Wingate.

The Jewish-Christian Alliance

Although I will speak about a new alliance between evangelical Christians and the Jewish people in another chapter, I feel it is incumbent to make an important point here. What these lives have said to us is that what we are witnessing today is nothing new. Since long before the rebirth of the modern State of Israel there has been an unshakable alliance between some Bible-believing Christians and some Bible-believing Jews. They have been inseparably linked in the cause of the return of the Jews to their homeland and the resurrection of the nation.

This is an alliance forged by the emergence of the returns—a return by evangelical Christians to a literal, historical interpretation of the prophetic Scriptures regarding Israel, and the return of an insatiable desire among Jews to again claim their ancient homeland. In these respects the returns have converged. They have converged and cooperated in one of the greatest national enterprises ever seen on the face of the planet.

What we are witnessing today in America, I believe, is that old alliance taking on a new dimension. It is, if you will, a maturing of relationships. Perhaps it is being pressed upon us, as in the Holocaust experience, by a certain environment-borne desperation. Nonetheless, it is there. And it is a phenomenon that must be nurtured rather than discouraged.

7

An Evangelical View of the Jew

For years we had waited for one of our children—three boys and one girl—to bring a granddaughter into our lives. We had five wonderful grandsons, each one special in his own way. A granddaughter, however, would bring to our lives that very special dimension that only little girls can provide. We communicated our eagerness to friends, who during the pregnancy of one of our daughters-in-law presented us with a pink Polly Flinders dress. But the baby was a boy, and that frilly pink dress hung in our closet for nearly ten years before the much-desired granddaughter finally put in an appearance.

Our daughter Melissa became pregnant, and through the wonder of sonogram we learned that our newest grandchild was to be a girl.

Initial exuberance, however, was dashed a bit when we

learned that the baby had an irregularity in her heart that was causing Missy's doctors some concern. As could be expected, our anxiety was acute.

The prescribed treatment, administered through our daughter's body, was the drug digitalis. Following a successful birth, Brooke was treated with digitalis for another six months. Today she is doing well and brings more pleasure than we could have anticipated as she spins her little webs around our hearts.

As a grandfather, I can speak for an entire family that is profoundly grateful to God for granting a Jewish scientist the skill to discover the drug that helped preserve her life and enrich ours.

Henry Ford and the Jews

As we have seen, across the centuries certain people have sought to rid the world of the Jew. Even today, with anti-Semitism on the rise, we are hearing voices that denigrate the Jewish people or seek ways to finish the macabre work of demonically inspired men like Adolf Hitler. In the twisted world of the anti-Semite, the Jewish people have been accused of creating or contributing to every vice that has plagued humanity.

As a young man I worked for a time at Greenfield Village in Dearborn, Michigan. It was a delightful experience in a place filled with antiques and marvelous relics from an America that once was. In the rooms above the museum, which were not open to the public, were many of the personal belongings of the Ford family. I was fascinated by the shelves full of books that I presumed had been the personal library of Henry Ford himself, so I sometimes thumbed through the selections with a sense of being in touch with the man who had changed the direction and driving habits of the nation.

On those shelves I found volumes on subjects strange to me. I had never heard much about nor read books on reincarnation—a belief I understand was held by Mr. Ford. Some of the books revealed a man I had not known existed. When I was a child, Henry Ford was to me the man of the wonderful machine that was very much a part of our lives. Many members of my family worked in the factories that were part of the Ford auto empire.

In that library, however, I met Henry Ford the anti-Semite—a person who held strong sympathies for the views of Adolf Hitler in matters touching the Jew, Zionism, and the so-called "international Jewish conspiracy."

Mr. Ford published his views in his newspaper, *The Dearborn Independent,* and later compiled some 91 articles from the *Independent* in four volumes titled *The International Jew: The World's Foremost Problem.* The core of those books was *The Protocols of the Learned Elders of Zion,* which he used as a basis for blaming conspiratorial "Jewish Elders" for a wide range of problems, including the Russian Revolution.

Jews were blamed for amusement parks like Coney Island, which he called "centers of nervous thrills and looseness." "Sports clothes and flashy jewelry" were Jewish devices used to corrupt Americans. Even jazz, according to Ford, was not an African-American invention but rather "Yiddish moron music."

But beyond espousing this type of thinking, Henry Ford articulated some basic accusations that have pervaded the thinking of anti-Semites historically and are being relentlessly parroted by some people even today.

The Jewish international conspiracy: Christopher Columbus was an illustration of the conspiracy.

The story of the Jews in America begins with Christopher Columbus. On August 2, 1492, more than 300,000 Jews were expelled

from Spain....On August 3, the next day,
Columbus set sail for the West, taking a group
of Jews with him....Columbus himself tells us
that he consorted much with Jews...the event-
ful voyage itself was made possible by Jews....
There were three Marranos or "secret Jews"
who wielded great influence at the Spanish
Court....Associated with Columbus on the
voyage were at least five Jews....Columbus
himself became the victim of a conspiracy fostered by [the Jew] Bernal...and suffered injus-
tice and imprisonment as his reward.[29]

Jewish domination of international business: Judaism, in
Ford's scheme of things, was a front for unsavory business
practices.

It is not his religion that gives prominence
to the Jew today; it is something else....
Business to the Jewish mind is money; what the
successful Jew may do with his money after he
gets it is another matter, but in the getting of
it, he never permits "idealistic slush" to inter-
fere with the dollar....

In America alone most of the big businesses, the trusts and the banks, the national
resources and chief agricultural products,
especially tobacco, cotton and sugar, are in
control of Jewish financiers or their agents.[30]

Jews always stick together:

The American Jew does not assimilate....
The International Jew...rules not because he
is rich, but because in a most marked degree

he...avails himself of a racial loyalty and solidarity the like of which exists in no other
human groups....Gentiles have not the basis
either in blood or interest that the Jews have to
stand together.... [T]here is a lacking in the
Gentile, a certain quality of working-together-
ness, a certain conspiracy of objective and
adhesiveness of intense raciality which charac-
terizes the Jew.[31]

Jews are warmongers motivated by greed:

"Wars are the Jews' harvest" is an ancient
saying....American Jews...have failed to
make known to the American public the information which may be found in the Jewish
archives concerning [the traitor] Benedict
Arnold....Did international Jews in 1903 foresee the [world] war? This...confession is but
one bit of evidence that they did. And did they
do nothing but foresee it? It were well if the
facts stopped and did not run on to provoca-
tion.... [Quoting *Protocol* 7, Jewish Elders sup-
posedly plotting against humanity] "To each
act of opposition we must be in a position to
respond by bringing on war through the
neighbors of any country that dares oppose us,
and if these neighbors should stand collectively
against us, we must let loose world war."[32]

Jews oppress Gentiles:

Here...is something for Jewish religious
leaders to consider: There is more downright
bitterness of religious prejudice on the part of

Jews against Christians than could ever be possible in the Christian churches of America.... This doctrine of the usefulness of anti-Semitism and the desirability of creating it where it does not exist are found in the words of Jewish leaders, ancient and modern.[33]

These themes are as old as anti-Semitism and make the Jewish people the authors of their own millennia-long miseries, as well as sponsors of virtually every woe befalling Gentiles. To see these ideas propagated by men at the level of prominence of Henry Ford is difficult for reasonable people to comprehend. Compounding the problem is the fact that there is a kind of insidious succession once such ideas are embraced and propagated by otherwise distinguished people.

The case of Henry Ford is a prime example. He has been named as the "spiritual godfather" of Louis Farrakhan, one of this generation's most notorious anti-Semites and one who follows the Ford assertions against Jews almost point by point.

A World Without Jews?

But what of a world without Jews?

That Jewish people are prone to sin, like the rest of us, is not at issue. Their 613 commandments, or *mitzvoth*, only serve to demonstrate the inevitability of stepping across the line. In evangelical terms, this is "missing the mark" of God's required standard for righteousness. Evangelicals believe and history lavishly documents what Scripture declares—namely, that "all have sinned, and come short of the glory of God" (Romans 3:23). So how do people who sin conduct themselves?

Like all people affected by the fall, that's how—no exceptions. It is a human frailty that is not the exclusive province of Jews, as anti-Semites would have us believe. Nor are Jews, as a people, guilty of the preposterous crimes against humanity of which they are accused by some, like Henry Ford, who should have known better.

It is no more rational to hold Jewry guilty of the transgressions of a few than it would be to indict the entire Ford family or the Ford Motor Company for the warped personal views of their father and the founder of the company.

The temptation to sin is a universal affliction. While Gentiles have had their Al Capones, Jews have undeniably had their "Bugsy" Segals. But be assured that the Jewish people take no more pride in the "Bugsy" Segals of Jewry than Gentiles do in the Al Capones who have stained the pages of American history.

Those of us who support Israel are sometimes accused of having an "Israel, right or wrong" kind of loyalty. That is, Israel can do no wrong. This, of course, is patently nonsense. Israel is a secular government, just as the government of the United States is a secular government. Do secular governments make mistakes and sometimes make wrong decisions? Indeed they do. But this does not negate the fact that Israel has a right to exist, and that Christians have a divine mandate to stand by this right and the related rights of the Jewish people.

What would we all have lost had God not called out a special people when He, in Abraham, created the first Hebrew? I previously quoted from Romans on the matter of sin and sinners. The apostle Paul also had something to say about the Jewish legacy that all believers enjoy today.

Speaking of his kinsmen, Paul said, "Who are Israelites; to whom pertaineth the adoption, and the glory, and the covenants, and the giving of the law, and the service of God, and the promises; whose are the fathers, and of whom, as concerning the flesh, Christ came, who is over all, God blessed forever. Amen" (Romans 9:4,5).

In other words, what has been given to us through Jewry is not a marginal asset; it comprises the core of the faith we possess, an essence of the indispensable aspects of our spiritual heritage. If we extract the Jew from history, here are some of the facts we would face.

- A Jewless world would be a pagan world, laced with every vice that Christians repudiate.
- A Jewless world would be a world devoid of the undergirding of God's guiding Word. Remember that in addition to the Old Testament, all the New Testament writers with one possible exception were Jewish.
- A Jewless world would be a world without the Mosaic Law upon which our system of laws and social order has been constructed. We are witnessing at this moment the deterioration of respect for our Judeo-Christian system of laws, and as a result the prospects for the future run directly toward anarchy.
- A Jewless world would be void of the standards for moral conduct restraining mankind's worst proclivities. It was through biblical Judaism that we were given a basis for proper moral conduct. Short of that standard, we would live in a world where, as in the days of the Judges, when men deviated from divine standards, "every man did that which was right in his own eyes" (Judges 17:6; 21:25).
- A Jewless world would be a world that suppressed women. Judaism, and subsequently Christianity, freed women from the pagan chatteldom still in effect in many cultures. When we see, for example, a Bedouin's tent separated to house his four wives, and perhaps a few more sections for those he has divorced and is still

obligated to support, we learn very quickly the value of the Judeo-Christian standards for women.

- A Jewless world would be a world without Christ. Beyond the fact that He was unquestionably born of a Jewish mother, if you make Jesus the product of any pagan Gentile culture of the period, you face a serious dilemma. Apart from the prophecies and mores of biblical Judaism, there is no basis upon which to claim messiahship. Christianity would not have been Christianity, for Christ (*Anointed One*) is a name found in a messianic context in Judaism alone.
- Consequently, a Jewless world would be a world with neither Judeo-Christian values and standards of conduct nor a cohesive moral and ethical society.
- A Jewless world would be a world with the lights out.

Could God have chosen to do things another way? Most certainly. But He didn't. He brought into the world a Chosen People, thoroughly human—ordinary, if you will—but through them He chose to do extraordinary things, and we are all beneficiaries of the marvel that is the Jew.

It is striking indeed to see that every anti-Semitic group or movement attempts to separate Christ from His Jewish origins. To the Nazis and all of their ilk He has been transformed into an Aryan. To Palestinians He has been transformed into a Palestinian freedom fighter. To Black Muslims He has become a Black Jesus. And for assorted cultists Jesus has been molded into whatever their particular religious perversity would make Him.

Separate Him from biblical Judaism and He becomes but another product of some exploitive provincial movement. In other words, Jesus is converted into a tool of convenience—transformed into a teacher of things inexplicable if they are unrelated to the Torah and not woven into the great fabric of the Old Testament messianic prophecies.

Jewish Contributions

In all that has been said and written by people with a dislike for Jewish people, there is one overwhelmingly striking feature: We search in vain to find a single admission that Jews have contributed anything of worth to the human condition. Even the most biased biographers will, however grudgingly, admit to some virtuous elements in the characters about whom they write. Mafia dons, for example, are usually credited with being considerate family men.

I suppose it could be said that admitting Jewish people "stick together," although it is portrayed as something ominous, is a kind of backhanded compliment. After all, that is a virtue commended by Christ and set forth as a mandate for Christians. Loving one another, caring for indigent brethren, and looking after widows and orphans are among the specific commands of the New Testament as well the Old. So in truth Jewish people cannot be faulted for assisting one another.

This fact aside, there are no commendable attributes ascribed to Jewry by anti-Semites.

However, it is an incontestable fact that no people on earth have made more constructive contributions to the welfare of humanity than have the Jewish people. Considering that they are but a minute sliver of the world's population, and then scaling their contributions, it is simply astonishing. It goes without saying that those who defame Jews are not hesitant to avail themselves and members of their families to what Jewish people have made possible.

Haym Salomon

It was a Jew, Haym Salomon, who played a major role in helping the young republic of the United States of America, struggling to become an independent nation, survive at its birth. The Polish-born, idealistic financier, who combined wealth with an unselfish loyalty to his principles, was largely responsible for the financial survival of the new nation.

His lavish grants for the payment of George Washington's soldiers and his underwriting of the country's financial commitments enabled the United States to weather the storm of those early days.

No gain came to Salomon or his descendants, however. So complete was his commitment to the young republic that he was left a financially ruined man.

Chaim Weizman

Some 150 years later another Jew, Chaim Weizman, would step in to help the cause of freedom and indirectly save the lives of thousands of Allied troops. Weizman, who would later become the State of Israel's first President, was a renowned chemist. At Manchester University in England he isolated a starch-decomposing organism that produced acetone. The discovery was a boon to the British during World War I, because their munitions required enormous amounts of acetone. Weizman's contribution helped bring about a successful conclusion to "the war to end all wars," and the Western world was secured for freedom.

Jonas Salk and Albert Sabin

Jewish contributions in the field of medicine alone are something for which every Gentile in the civilized world should be deeply grateful.

The elimination of the threat of polio is an extremely graphic example. I can recall as a child the fears that came with each summer season, and the thought that some of us children would fall prey to the dreaded malady. President Franklin Roosevelt was a constant reminder of the devastating effects of the disease.

Jewish epidemiologist, Jonas Salk, who recently died while seeking a vaccine for AIDS, developed the first vaccine against poliomyelitis. The New York-born Salk's vaccine virtually eliminated polio, which had reached epidemic proportions since the beginning of the twentieth century.

Albert Sabin, a Jewish virologist born in Poland, developed the live oral polio vaccine that went into mass use in 1961 and almost eliminated the disease around the world.

Waldemar Haffkine

After working under Pasteur in Paris, Haffkine discovered the method of inoculation against cholera. In 1893, at the invitation of the Indian government, he went to India to conduct a campaign against bubonic plague, which was then killing vast numbers of people in India. At the risk of his own life, Haffkine continued his work and discovered a method of inoculation that reduced the mortality by over 80 percent.

It is ironic that a Jew would be the instrument used in saving hundreds of thousands of people from the plague which his own people were accused of spreading in medieval Europe.

Fernand Widal

This Algerian-born French Jew impacted the world of medicine in 1896 by discovering a method for diagnosing and preventing typhoid fever. His method became a prototype for diagnosing other communicable diseases. His most important contribution was his recognition that sodium in table salt causes water retention. He instituted the now universally used low-salt diet in cases of fluid retention.

Bela Schick

Schick, a Hungarian-American Jewish pediatrician, discovered a method for determining susceptibility to diphtheria, an acutely contagious disease mainly afflicting children. For many years it was one of the most serious diseases in the world. The Schick test, developed in 1913, brought a remarkable victory in preventive medicine and placed diphtheria in the category of vanishing diseases.

Selman Abraham Waksman

Waksman coined the term *antibiotic* in 1941. Born in the Ukraine, he served as head of Rutgers University Institute of Microbiology. In 1944 Waksman discovered the antibiotic streptomycin, which became the first effective medicine to treat and control tuberculosis. He won the Nobel prize for medicine in 1952. He also isolated and developed several other antibiotics, including neomycin.

The Anti-Semite's Dilemma

The list of Jewish contributors and their contributions to the physical well-being of all of us seems endless. Perhaps a fitting summary—one certainly in keeping with the themes of this book—was given by a non-Jewish physician, Dr. Lukatchewsky, depicting the quandary of a conscientious anti-Semite who refuses to avail himself of any remedy invented by Jews—in this case, Nazis.

> A Nazi who has a venereal disease must not allow himself to be cured by Salvarsan, because it is the discovery of the Jew Ehrlich. He must not even take steps to find out

whether he has this ugly disease, because the Wasserman reaction that is used for the purpose is the discovery of a Jew. A Nazi who has heart disease must not use digitalis, the medical use of which was discovered by the Jew Ludwig Traube. If he has a toothache, he will not use cocaine, or he will be benefiting by the work of a Jew, Carl Koller. Typhoid must not be treated, or he will have to benefit by the discoveries of the Jews Vidal and Weil. If he has diabetes, he must not use insulin, because its invention was made possible by the research work of the Jew Minkowsky. If he has a headache, he must shun pyramidon and antipyrin (Spiro and Eilege). Anti-Semites who have convulsions must put up with them, for it was a Jew, Oscar Liebreich, who thought of chloral-hydrate.[34]

Then there was the Jewess Emma Lazarus. She was born in New York City and championed the cause of the oppressed. Although she penned many poems, her best known is *The New Colossus*, which graces the base of the Statue of Liberty and is now inscribed at Kennedy International Airport.

Her immortal words, written on a single sheet of paper, express a vision of America that will linger always in the hearts of its immigrants.

> Give me your tired, your poor,
> Your huddled masses yearning to breathe free,
> The wretched refuse of your teaming shore.
> Send these, the homeless, tempest tossed, to me.
> I lift my lamp beside the golden door.

I Am a Debtor

Interesting words, these. The apostle Paul, referring to his burden to deliver his message, said, "I am debtor both to the Greeks and to the barbarians, both to the wise and to the unwise" (Romans 1:14). It is an admirable statement of dedication to his mission and a sterling principle for all of us to live by.

Today most evangelicals with whom I travel feel a sense of gratitude and indebtedness for what has passed to us from the Jewish people, the Book, and the heritage recorded earlier in this chapter. When we think of the riches that have accrued to us through the revelation—by way of the Chosen People—of "the glory, and the covenants, and the giving of the law and the promises," we should have a profound feeling of appreciation.

Of course, for evangelical Christians the consummating consideration is found in the phrase "and of whom, as concerning the flesh, Christ came."

Evangelicals have no question that Jesus of Nazareth was a Jew. When properly seen, this impacts dramatically His view of the Scriptures and how they should be interpreted. In a previous chapter we discussed the premillennial theology that gives Israel and Jewish people the place properly appointed them by God. Recognizing that Christ was brought to us as a Jew buttresses the concept that, if this is true, the Scriptures can be best understood by studying them through the historical and cultural context in which they were given.

There was a reason why Jesus was a Jew. Therefore, it is vital to view His life and hear His teachings through the prism of His people, the culture in which they lived, and above all His associations with the Old Testament Scriptures and the great festive commemorations that were at the heart of the religious and social life of the nation.

I have heard Jewish people complain from time to time that Christians have so "Gentilized" their approach to the Scriptures that they find little related to the Jewish people in Christian teaching. Unfortunately, in much of Protestantism this is true. It is also true that certain Protestants hold significant misconceptions about some of the teachings in the New Testament itself.

Evangelicals understand that God's stated purposes for Israel and Jewry are irrevocable, that Jesus came to us as a Jew, and that He was careful to address us from a Jewish frame of reference. Once we see this, it seems inevitable that we should sense kinship and appreciation for the Jewish people.

In saying this, I am not romanticizing about the Jewish people. Nor am I implying superior and inferior positioning of one people above another. The Scriptures make it clear that God did not choose the children of Abraham because they were more in number than or inordinately superior to their neighbors.

> Thou art an holy people unto the LORD thy God; the LORD thy God hath chosen thee to be a special people unto himself, above all people who are upon the face of the earth.
>
> The LORD did not set his love upon you, nor choose you, because ye were more in number than any people, for ye were the fewest of all people.
>
> But because the LORD loved you, and because he would keep the oath which he had sworn unto your fathers, hath the LORD brought you out with a mighty hand, and redeemed you out of the house of bondage, from the hand of Pharaoh, king of Egypt (Deuteronomy 7:6-8).

But, He insists, if not inherently superior, the Jewish people are nevertheless *chosen*, and through them we are the beneficiaries of His gifts to the world.

In my experience as a Christian, I learned early on to appreciate the prophetic portions of the Scriptures—the "promises." Thus when I became a minister I often brought sermons from the Old Testament. One evening while speaking to a congregation in another town I was discussing a passage from the book of Isaiah. When I finished, a man approached me before I could leave the platform. He was obviously quite upset.

Laying his hand on my Bible, he said, "Young man, where does the Bible begin for you?"

"Why, with Genesis 1:1, of course," I replied.

"That's where you are all wrong," he shot back.

"You are a Christian, and for you the Bible begins with the first verse of the book of Matthew."

As a young and rather inexperienced minister, I realized I was looking into the irate face of a spiritually deprived man, and perhaps one who had a less–than–favorable attitude toward the children of Abraham.

Those who share his sentiments are equally deprived.

The National Christian Prayer Breakfast in Honor of Israel

For well over a decade, evangelicals have been publicly expressing solidarity with the State of Israel and the Jewish people at a prayer breakfast held in conjunction with the annual meeting of the National Religious Broadcasters. The event was conceived and is led by Ed McAteer, founder of the Religious Roundtable.

Each year the event has grown in numbers and stature as leading evangelicals, members of the Jewish community, and dignitaries from the Israeli and United States governments come together. The breakfasts have usually been held in Washington D.C., but in recent years other cities have hosted the event, including the city of Jerusalem in Israel.

These are impressive gatherings, and it seems that each one leaves something special to be taken home and remembered. For example, of all the speeches made by leading dignitaries—Christian and Jewish—at the breakfast in Jerusalem, I remember most vividly a two-minute talk made by Irvin Borowsky, a prominent Jewish businessman from Philadelphia. He expressed his appreciation for evangelical Christians by saying that his feelings were very personal. In 1903, in Russia, his parents were hidden by Christians beneath straw in a wagon and taken to safety during a bloody pogrom. I was deeply touched by his words.

I have had the privilege of speaking at these events for the past several years, and I have noticed an evolution of sorts taking place. Ed McAteer and I, along with others, were particularly impressed by this at the breakfast held in Memphis, Tennessee, in 1993.

Approximately 1500 people filled the hall and overflow rooms at the Peabody Hotel in downtown Memphis. Among the large Jewish contingent attending were 50 honored guests—Holocaust survivors. Their presence perhaps enhanced the tone of the meeting and the sensitivity of the Christians present. But even apart from this there was something extemely impressive about the gathering.

The essence of the quality of the Memphis breakfast was summed up in two statements made by Jewish people who attended. One was made by a Holocaust survivor.

"I did not know," she said, "that such people as this existed.

"In all of my life, I have never experienced such an outpouring of unconditional love."

The other was expressed during a visit several months later with a prominent Israeli friend in Jerusalem, who also spoke at the event. We had been together for several of these affairs and were chatting about the Memphis meeting. We agreed that it had been a bit different from previous breakfasts.

"Do you know what I think it was?" he asked.

I was, of course, curious.

"I think it was because there was not a feeling of being there as two camps—eyeing each other with a bit of suspicion.

"The feeling seemed to be one of unity; we sat together as friends."

And so it should be.

At that breakfast, as is always true, no evangelical went undercover about his or her faith. Nor was any Jewish participant the less Jewish. But there was a sense of camaraderie—a bridging, if you will, that seemed to bring us to the common ground we share because of who we are.

Perhaps this attitude is a natural outgrowth of the threat that both communities are feeling from an increasingly hostile culture. Maybe significant segments of the Jewish and evangelical communities are beginning to appreciate how much we have in common and are seeing reasons why we should strengthen our relationships.

Or it may just be that God is doing something on both sides of the line "for such a time as this."

8

The Hate Merchants

He that toucheth you [Israel] toucheth the apple of his [God's] eye.
—Zechariah 2:8

As we have seen, in the past evangelicals and Jews have had an alliance in two fundamental areas. The first area, that regarding Israel's rebirth and preservation, has been the most obvious. Not as highly profiled, but with insidious global potential, has been anti-Semitism.

A biblical mandate has been issued to evangelicals to take seriously the scriptural admonitions regarding the Jewish people. The verse that projects the entire tenor of the Bible on this matter is quoted above: *Don't take it upon yourselves,* all people are warned, *to touch in a malicious way these people called "the apple of his eye."* In the event they need correction, God is perfectly capable of handling that matter

149

Himself. The principle is very simple: A father is responsible for correcting his son. It is not left to neighbors, or even friends of the family, to do so.

However, contrary to clear biblical teaching, and against any rational justification, a procession reaching back into the mists of antiquity has seemed more than eager to violate the divine mandate by afflicting Jewish people. Pagans, Muslims, and pseudo-Christians have traipsed across the stage of human history, equipped with the paraphernalia of death and destruction, bent on slaughtering the Jewish people and destroying Israel.

I use the term *pseudo-Christians* because it is beyond comprehension that any biblically literate Christian would line up against the Jewish people. Sad to say, some, however, have been duped into doing so, even though the overwhelming sentiment of evangelicals today runs firmly in the opposite direction.

A rather homely little poem written by Will Houghton, a former president of the Moody Bible Institute in Chicago, expresses things pretty well when it comes to true Christians and the Jew.

> Say not a Christian e'er would
>   persecute a Jew;
> A Gentile might, but not a Christian true.
>   Pilate and Roman guard that folly tried.
> And with that great Jew's death, an empire died!
>
> When Christians gather in a cathedral,
>   church, or hall,
> Hearts turn toward One—the name of Jesus call.
>   You cannot persecute—whatever else you do—
> That race that gave Him—Jesus was a Jew!

Moving into a Third Dimension

Today we are rapidly moving beyond the old-line anti-Semitism that has characterized the past several centuries. There is a new face on the dark phenomenon that takes us beyond the realm of the Jew. For Americans it has exploded in the cultural confrontation that is polarizing the nation. The so-called and much maligned Religious Right is being spun by secular humanists into a tapestry of dangerous patterns that threaten to smother individual freedoms and the social liberation won by radicals in the Woodstock era. Now that sixties-driven paganism has settled into the American mainstream and is dignified in the highest offices of the land, cultural battle lines have been drawn.

The face-off is between those who hold to the traditional Judeo-Christian values upon which the country was built and the new-wave hedonists bent on crafting a creature-centered Utopia—one that is free from the inhibiting strictures of divine absolutes. The result is a brand of discrimination previously unknown in this country. We are actually witnessing a reversal of historic cultural values, and those bent on imposing the new system have zero tolerance for any opposing voices. It is, if I may coin a phrase, *anti-Judeo/Christianism*. Although the term may be a bit cumbersome, it is accurate. Jews who hold to traditional values are framed in the crosshairs with conservative Christians who adhere to the same basic values.

So evangelical Christians and conservative Jews find themselves within this third dimension. It was not created by either group but rather is being imposed upon us by imperialistic humanists eager to have things their way. Whether or not everyone is comfortable with this new phrase describing our new alliance, it has arrived, and with it the harbingers of some possibly very dark days down the line.

Several months ago I had a conversation with a Jewish friend whom I consider a man of unusual perception. We were discussing the burgeoning alliance between evangelical Christians and the growing body of politically conservative Jews. I asked, "Why is it difficult to make the case to some Jewish people that evangelicals have a genuine love for Jews and Israel, and that their love is unconditional?"

"That's just it," he countered. "Many Jewish people have a hard time accepting the fact that Christians would love them without some element of self-interest involved."

I've done a considerable amount of thinking about that concept and now believe I understand what he meant. The way things now seem to be heading, there is a vested self-interest for evangelicals in standing against anti-Semitic thrusts directed at Jews. Our interest is in the fact that we are now also targeted by some elements in our society as undesirables—people making religious war against those crafting a new cultural agenda.

I'm afraid that when we examine radical Muslim motives for reckoning with infidels—Jews and Christians—we are going to find an insidious parallel expression in Western society. It is a strategy that strikes at the Jew first, then at conservative Christians, who are also considered obstructionists.

This being true, Jewish people become a sort of first line of defense for Christians. Therefore it is indeed in our best interest to stand, with every fiber of our beings, against anti-Semitism. If Jewish people can see this as a reason for evangelical solidarity with them, I suppose it is a step in the right direction. But the fact remains that whether some Jewish friends ever fully comprehend it, there is a vast host of Bible-believing evangelicals who love Jews just because they are Jews.

We will come back to the developing alliance between politically conservative Jews and evangelicals later, but first let's look into some of the faces of old—line anti-Semites.

The Nazis Are Back

I was preparing to address a group of several hundred people in Greensboro, North Carolina, when I was approached by a colleague who looked rather worried.

"I have something to tell you before you speak," she said.

"Okay, what is it?" I replied.

"I can't tell you here. Will you please step out into the hall?"

Wondering what this was all about, I complied.

"I thought you should know that there is a neo-Nazi in the crowd."

"Well, good," I said. "I'm going to say some things I would like him to hear."

My co-worker still looked worried.

"But we're afraid of what he may be planning to do."

Frankly, I was too, but I didn't want to betray my concerns to her and others.

"I'll tell you what to do," I instructed. "You stay near enough to him to keep an eye on what he does with his hands. That's what I'm most concerned about."

As the meeting began, I scanned the audience. I picked him out immediately; the young man was the only skinhead in the crowd. I thought as I sat there, *Here we are in the United States of America in 1994, and we're experiencing the thirties in Europe all over again.*

As astonishing as it may seem to rational people, the Nazi movement is making a comeback. In a report by Klanwatch, published in *Newsweek* on May 1, 1995, a map of the United States showed—coast to coast—some 80 swastikas. Those symbols represented separate neo-Nazi organizations, which, according to Klanwatch, may have multiple chapters within a state. Outnumbering the Nazis was the Ku Klux Klan, with nearly a hundred chapters, concentrated predominantly in the East, South, and Midwest. Thirty-five emblems represented militant skinhead organizations, with "others"—militias—numbering well over 60. To say that the presence of such groups is an ominous sign of the times is a point that both Christians and Jews had better pay attention to.

A Lesson from Latvia

What is happening to Jews in Latvia is a small sampling of what other Jews are, or may soon be, facing.

In late November 1941, the woods near Latvia's capital, Riga, became a killing ground. Over the course of two brutal weeks, 30,000 Jews from the Riga ghetto were marched into the woods, forced to strip before open death pits, and machine-gunned to death.

In no other country of Europe was the extermination of Jewish people so thorough. Of the 85,000 Jews living in Latvia at the time, only 500 survived the war.

Mira Beylina, six years old at the time, escaped by train to Russia in the middle of the night. When the war ended and Latvia was annexed by the Soviet Union, Mira returned home and attempted, with the remaining members of her family, to put the pieces of her life back together again. It was a relatively short-lived dream.

With the collapse of the Soviet Union, the "Old Warriors" from World War II donned their tattered uniforms once again and began training in the woods outside town. There they could be heard singing old German war songs and seen stiff-arming the Nazi salute. Two units of the "Old Warriors," former members of the SS Waffen, were allowed to join the Latvian Home Guard.

For Jews to see the same men—the ones who had marched their families into the woods to be killed—

strolling through the streets in their old swastika-pinned uniforms sent a chill through them. The handwriting was once again on the wall. Soon it was coming to them in neatly written pamphlet form.

"You must leave Latvian territory because you are here illegally. You will have to leave sooner or later. If you stay, you will provoke the forces of Latvia that are ready to solve the decolonization question by violent methods."

Mira's daughter, Leah, got the message by word of mouth on a bus.

"The conductor began screaming at me," she said tearfully. " 'Yid [Jew], you should all be killed; you must get out of Latvia.' "

In September 1994, Mira and her family boarded the train once again. With suitcases in hand, they were reliving an old nightmare, fleeing for the lives. Why? Because they are Jews.

The Christian Identity Mentality

Don't think for one minute that Western-style neo-Nazis are more benevolent or civilized than their goose-stepping Latvian comrades. Given the opportunity, their actions would carbon copy their European Nazi revivalists.

This conclusion is not drawn by imposed inferences; these people speak for themselves.

CNN Special Assignment Correspondent Kathy Slobogin did a series of interviews following the bombing of the Federal Building in Oklahoma City on April 19, 1995. She was looking into a possible link between members of the militantly anti-Semitic Christian Identity movement and the explosion that took 169 innocent lives. She learned that it is not known if Timothy McVeigh, the primary suspect in the bombing, is a Christian Identity believer. She did learn, however, that law enforcement sources said McVeigh had telephone contact with a

Christian Identity encampment a few days before the bombing.

An undercover investigator who infiltrates Christian Identity groups is quoted.

Kathy Slobogin: [Identity pastor] Barkley says neither he nor Christian Identity churches advocate violence. But we spoke to someone within the Identity movement who tells a different story.

Undercover Investigator: These are violent people. They have no reason to them. There's only one goal—that's white power to run the world.

Kathy Slobogin: What connection is there between the Oklahoma bombing and Christian Identity?

Undercover Investigator: Absolute connection. It came out of the Identity groups—positively.

The undercover investigator then played a tape he secretly recorded at a Christian Identity meeting in Branson, Missouri, two days after the bombing.

Kathy Slobogin: The mood of the Branson meeting confirmed this man's beliefs of an Oklahoma-Identity connection.

And why?

Undercover Investigator: The congratulations, the satisfaction of everyone.

Christian Identity Member: The thing is, you know, we're in a war. In a war you say—you know, there are casualties. That's what war is all about.

Kathy Slobogin: McVeigh—how is he viewed within the movement?

Undercover Investigator: As a hero. As a hero who expressed the rage of everybody in Identity for what happened in Waco. [35]

The investigator's conclusions will be confirmed or denied through future investigations, if indeed such investigations are forthcoming. There is no doubt, however— and that is the purpose of presenting a portion of the CNN interview in this space—that it captures concisely the malevolence of Christian Identity toward our government. When we examine Identity and its cohorts, we find an old specter that should strike fear into Jews and Christians, as well as law-abiding Americans.

Christian Identity is a loose network of organizations calling themselves churches. They are groups bearing names like The Aryan Nations; Covenant, Sword and Arm of the Lord; The Order; Arizona Patriots; Posse Comitatus; and an assortment of others. Today they number an estimated 30,000 adherents. And these people are no strangers to violence.

- 1983: Gordon Kahl, a tax rebel, killed two U.S. Marshals and wounded three others who had come to arrest him for nonpayment of taxes. Kahl, who was himself killed in a shootout with police, said taxes were "tithes to the synagogue of Satan."
- 1984: The Order declared war on the United States government. To members of Congress they wrote, "When the day comes, we will not ask whether you swung to the right or to the left. We will simply swing you by the neck."
- In a little over a year, their guerrilla warfare progressed from armed robbery to bombing a theater, burning a synagogue, and murder. Before they were finished, they had killed three people, including Alan Berg, a Jewish talkshow host. He was machine-gunned to death.
- 1985: A Covenant, Sword and Arm of the Lord encampment was raided. Federal agents recovered an

arsenal of automatic weapons, silencers, and grenades. The group's leader was convicted of manufacturing weapons, arson, and bombing a synagogue.

- 1988: Thirteen Identity leaders were prosecuted unsuccessfully for plotting to overthrow the government and attempting to set up an Aryan nation in the Pacific Northwest.
- 1992: Randy Weaver was charged with weapons violations by federal authorities. He and his family faced U.S. Marshals in a highly publicized 18-month standoff at Ruby Ridge near Naples, Idaho. Following an intensive ten-day siege, a series of shootings took the lives of a federal Marshal, Weaver's wife Vicki and his son Samuel.

Of all the Identity movement groups, Klanwatch calls The Aryan Nations "easily the most dangerous," and it is growing. Following a stage of apparent decline after the violence of the eighties, it began to expand its influence. In 1994 The Aryan Nations was reported to have spread from three to 18 states.

In 1994 one of the largest crowds of neo-Nazi skinheads in years attended Richard Butler's Aryan Nations Youth Festival, held at Hayden Lake, Idaho. About 150 skinheads and other white supremacists attended the Adolf Hitler birth celebration, up from only 25 in 1993.

With minor variations, all groups in the Identity movement hold to a pseudotheology that is as vicious as it is incoherent. All are white supremacists, espousing the British-Israel concept. A typical view is expressed in The Aryan Nations publication, *Calling Our Nation.*

> History says [our forefathers] came from
> the area between the Caspian and Black Seas.
> This is the area of the Caucasus Mountains

and explains why we are called the Caucasian Race. This is the same general area where the so-called "lost ten tribes" were taken as captives of the Assyrians in the eighth century B.C. (II Kings 17:5,6)....Our old Nordic ancestors probably came from their heritage of being a part of lost Israel, thus having a knowledge of God's Commandments, Statutes and Judgments given to Moses on Mt. Sinai.[36]

Identity groups also share in propagating *The Protocols of the Learned Elders of Zion* as a legitimate document. An Aryan Nations editorial quotes:

Protocol 9, Section 5...reads "It is from us [the Jews] that the all-engulfing terror proceeds. We have in our service persons of all opinions, of all doctrines, restoring monarchies, demagogues, socialists, communists and utopian dreamers of every kind. We have harnessed them all to our task [White destruction]."[37]

In the mentality of the Identity movement, the Jew is at the root of virtually every evil known to mankind. In the United States, the government is but a tool of the Zionists. "There is no United States of America," they say. "There is a centralized, one world worshipping federal power, a Zionist occupational government [ZOG in Identity terminology] which is imposed upon us" (from *The Mountain Newsletter*, July-August 1983).

Revisionists and Mel Mermelstein

The Identity movement also subscribes to the revisionist fiction that the Holocaust did not take place. It was the invention of devious Jewish plotters, who were themselves the perpetrators. An Identity author explains:

> The problem Jews faced was that there had been no holocausts of Jewish victims during World War II, nor were there any photographs of burned Jewish bodies. Not to worry—the Jews simply appropriated the photographs of the bodies of their German victims, which are exhibited today in gruesome "museums" in Germany as exhibits of dead Jews.[38]

Revisionists made the mistake of offering a $50,000-dollar reward for proof that "Jews were gassed in gas chambers at Auschwitz." A Holocaust survivor, Mel Mermelstein, took them up on the offer and sued the revisionist Institute of Historical Review, Liberty Lobby, and others. Mermelstein won his suit, and revisionists had to come up with the $50,000 dollars, pay another $50,000 dollars in damages, and issue a public apology as well.

It read:

> The Legion for Survival of Freedom, Institute for Historical Review, Noontide Press, Elizabeth Carto, Liberty Lobby, and Willis Carto do hereby officially and formally apologize to Mr. Mel Mermelstein, a survivor of Auschwitz-Birkenau and Buchenwald, and all other survivors of Auschwitz for the pain, anguish, and suffering he and all other Auschwitz survivors have sustained related to the $50,000 reward offer for proof that "Jews were gassed in the gas chambers in Auschwitz."[39]

Mark one up for judicial and historical sanity!

Identity Theology

Identity's general "theology" regarding race and the Jews is expressed in a booklet, *Racial and National Identity*, published by the Ministry of Christ Church, Mariposa, California. Author William P. Gale, an early organizer of the Identity movements, writes:

> Adam's entry on earth dates back some 7,400 years, yet there is sound scientific evidence that people existed on earth even 1,750,000 years ago. Carbon-14 tests have been applied to the bones of African blacks that have been found in the caves of Kilimanjaro, which date back approximately 73,000 years. There is also a history of Asiatic Sumerian dynasties which date back possibly 400,000 years or more. It is no wonder that many intelligent people who are aware of these archaeological and scientific findings, become skeptical of the Bible.... Having been taught by irresponsible clergy that all races of mankind descend from Adam and Eve, people do not have the facts and are unable to reconcile the findings of scientists and archaeologists, which prove that the earth was inhabited by Asiatics and Negroes long BEFORE the advent of Adam and Eve.... The Bible is not the history of ALL races. It is the history and guidebook of the WHITE RACE and begins with Adam.[40]

Thus Blacks and Asiatics are dealt out of the plans for the Aryan paradise. If Blacks and Asiatics are outside the veil, Jews fare even worse.

"He [Jesus] identified them as the offspring of Cain, who murdered Abel. Cain was the son of Eve's seduction by Satan, Cain was the progeny of 'that wicked one'.... This makes Cain the Son of Satan. It is from the Cain line that we have the so-called white Jew, Cain being the first of that type."

Gale further asserts, "The fall of Eve enabled Satan to place his children among us." The proof, according to this Identity "theologian," is in the words of Jesus. "Jesus was not speaking to His Own people when he made these accusations; for Jesus was NOT a Jew! He called them (the Jews) the children of Satan. Therefore, if He were one of them, He would be an offspring of Satan by His Own words." [41]

Have a Good Day

In *The Secret Holocaust, A Primer for the Aryan Nations Movement*, author Eustace Mullins states that Jewish employers have given Gentile employees specific instructions.

> ...They must greet each customer by saying "Have a good day." This apparently friendly and supposedly meaningless salutation lets the Jew in the know be tipped off that he is in a store owned by Jews, that the owners are anticipating "having a good day" in the future by more slaughters of the innocent and helpless Gentile women and children." [42]

Mullins goes on to indict Jews in the murder of millions.

> The figures are in, and they are indisputable; fifty million victims of World War I; a hundred and fifty million victims in World War II; sixty-six million Christians murdered

by Jewish fanatics in Russia....Many, if not the majority, of these victims of Jewish terrorism were women and children.[43]

Such demented thinking takes credulity to the outer limits, but the tragedy is that with modern technology and the tools to disseminate such devastatingly inflammatory gobbledygook, many of the disenchanted are buying in.

The young skinhead I spoke of early in this chapter is a textbook example. I talked with him at length after the Greensboro meeting. He had been an impressionable loner, searching for an identity. He found it within the neo-Nazis, who gave him the attention he apparently craved. He was indoctrinated by these people and programmed to believe the warped concepts quoted above. Finally, he felt, he had discovered his identity as a superior white warrior.

Spreading the Word

In 1985 The Aryan Nations unveiled its computer network. In promotional material they gloated:

> Imagine, if you can, a single computer that all the leaders and strategists of the patriotic movement are connected to. Imagine once again any patriot in the country being able to tap into this computer at will in order to reap the benefit of all the accumulative knowledge and wisdom of these leaders.[44]

The Aryans have used their computer network to advise others how to get on public access TV.

> There are 850 public access cable stations in the United States. No other method, activity

or campaign of any nature can match this avenue of propagation....What possible excuse could be given by an Aryan Nationalist for not going on the air if there is a cable network in his area?[45]

Identity views Christian ministers outside the movement only slightly more charitably than Blacks, Asiatics, and Jews. Statements such as "Satan rules Christian churches as the anti-Christ" and references to preachers as "these modern day, anti-Christ 'Christians'...proclaiming world Jewry as the Messiah" lace Identity literature.

A speaker at a rally for embattled farmers who were losing farms in the Midwest during the mid-eighties had this to say about their ministers: "You wonder why you're losing your farms and ranches and businesses out there? Because your minister has lied to you concerning a bunch of international Communist Jews that have stripped your wealth and your land from you" (ABC report, *20/20*, August 15, 1985).

This type of doctrine and venomous rhetoric is common fare among various branches of the white supremacy groups. Cross-burning Klansmen, swastika-bearing neo-Nazi foot soldiers with their skinheads, and individual renegade anti-Semites revel in their belligerence and anti-establishment notoriety. Most disturbing is that, like David Koresh, they have adopted an Armageddon complex, and, to make matters worse, many of them are armed and dangerous.

A man named George Stout, identified as The Aryan Nations' Texas leader, in an article titled "Apocalypse Now" issues a chilling challenge:

We cannot overthrow the government of Satan by voting or demonstrating against it....

The era of the persecuted martyrs is over. From now on let martyrs die with a rifle in their hand. It is the unarmed pacifist who will be persecuted, and the Identity movement has its fill of organizations wishing to be persecuted and annihilated. In this world of strife and turmoil, he who will not fight does not deserve to live.

You as an Israelite must prepare for the hardships to come....Aryan Warriors, do not turn away from your duty. Do not worry about the final tribulations. Face them with your head held high, with the praise of Yahweh on your lips, and an assault rifle in your hands.[46]

Prepared to Fight

Since the tragic bombing of the Federal Building in Oklahoma City, attention has been turned on the numbers of military militias training at various locations across the country. Theirs is a rather murky world. While many disavow active relationships with movements like Identity, they are preparing to fight. Their leaders do not make it clear just whom they are preparing to make war with; nonetheless, they are ready for armed conflict. The least we can say is that such manifestations in America are not contributing to a tranquil attitude about the future.

Louis Farrakhan and the Nation of Islam

Among the most dangerous negative elements in America's racially charged society today is Louis Farrakhan and the Nation of Islam. Farrakhan's influence goes far beyond the estimated 20,000 members of his movement. A *Time* magazine poll has revealed that 60 to 70 percent of African-Americans consider Farrakhan "an effective leader" "who speaks the truth," is "good for the Black community," and "says things the country should hear."

Knowing something about this man "who speaks the truth" and the version of "truth" he speaks shows just how vulnerable some people are to the rhetoric of hate and the volatile potential it can produce.

The Black Muslim Movement

It is important to note that Farrakhan's brand of Islam is not yet a dominant force in the American Muslim movement. Black Muslims, a rapidly growing group, number more than one million—nearly a third of the Muslim population of the United States. They worship in 200 mosques in 41 states.

The Black Muslim movement was founded in 1931 in Detroit by Elijah Poole, a factory worker from Georgia, and Wallace Fard, a salesman. The two organized the "Lost-Found Nation of Islam." Poole changed his name to Elijah Muhammad and began preaching a mixture of Islam and black nationalism that depicted the white man as Satan.

Malcolm X, who broke with Elijah Muhammad to seek a more orthodox Islam, was killed by religious rivals.

After Elijah Muhammad's death in 1975, his son and successor, Warith Deen Muhammad, renounced the racist and non-Islamic doctrines of his father and began a move to bring American Black Muslims under the mantle of orthodox Islam.

In 1978 Saudi Arabia, Abu Dhabi, and Qatar hailed the movement's return to orthodoxy and officially recognized Warith Muhammad as the head of American Black Muslims. Five years later he virtually disbanded the organization, and the movement was absorbed into the larger body of orthodox Islam (*U.S. News and World Report*, October 8, 1990, p. 71).

Nation of Islam

To say that the Nation of Islam's teachings do not square with mainstream Islam is putting it mildly.

At their 1991 "Savior's Day" celebration, Nation of Islam followers heard this answer to a fundamental question:

> Who is the present manifestation of Allah? ...Louis Farrakhan was introduced as the fulfillment of Isaiah 9:6-8. He was proclaimed as the "child who would be born" and the "son who would be given" because he was "Wonderful, Counselor, the Prince of Peace," etc.!
>
> It was stated that Farrakhan healed the sick and made the blind to see. It was implied clearly that Farrakhan was now "God manifested in the flesh." [47]

This teaching, though shocking to more biblically attuned minds, is not new to Farrakhan's brand of Islam. In point 12 of the organization's statement of faith, printed on the back of their newspaper, *The Final Call*, it is stated:

"We believe that Allah (God) appeared in the Person of Master W. Fard Muhammad, July 1930, the long-awaited 'Messiah' of the Christians and the 'Mahdi' of the Muslims" (I.I. 167).

When Fard died, "God then manifested himself in Elijah Muhammad who was revealed to be the long-awaited 'Messiah' of the Jews, the 'Jesus' of the Christians, and the 'Mahdi' of the Muslims!" (I.I. 168).

Farrakhan's stated goal for himself and his followers is to set up a separate Nation of Islam with its own military and justice system.

The dark side of the "Nation's" intentions was heard in a statement videotaped at the 1991 "Savior's Day" celebration.

The head of Farrakhan's "army" stated that he was tired of hearing people say that they were willing to die for Islam.

What he wanted to know was if they were willing to kill for Islam. The time is coming, he said, when they must kill all that is white, that is not right.[48]

Radical Connections

That Farrakhan has welcomed associations with radical Islamic regimes is well-known. His 1984 speeches labeling Judaism as "a gutter religion" and Adolf Hitler as "a great man" catapulted him into the national spotlight. It also brought him and his movement to the attention of Libya's Muammar al-Qaddafi, who showed his appreciation to Farrakhan's radicalism by presenting him with a gift of $5 million dollars. Farrakhan demonstrated his appreciation by standing with Qaddafi in backing Saddam Hussein during the Gulf War.

In November 1992, "Farrakhan accepted an invitation to speak at a conference in Stockholm, canceled at the last minute by the Swedish government, of anti-'Zionist' Holocaust deniers including members of the Russian fascist Pamyat as well as Hezbollah and Hamas from the Middle East" (*Ministry of Lies*, pp. 109-10).

Nation of Islam and the Jews

Farrakhan's most vicious attacks are reserved for the Jews, who are blamed for everything from running the slave trade and inventing AIDS to polluting Europe's lungs with tobacco, Asia's bloodstream with opium, and the American Indians' blankets with smallpox.

To dignify his irrational tirades against Jewish people, Farrakhan has produced a "scholarly" work, the Nation of Islam's *The Secret Relationship Between Blacks and Jews*. The book, as it turns out, is Farrakhan's version of *The Protocols of the Learned Elders of Zion*. The book duplicates the catalog of lies found in the *Protocols*.

At the Harvard Foundation for Intercultural and Race Relations, Chuck D. Muhammad told a Jewish member of the audience, "You and your people have a history of crime in America as long as the highways of America." Among "the crimes against humanity" of which Jews were accused was "the hole in the ozone layer." Although that bizarre accusation may cause people to chuckle a bit, there is nothing to laugh about in Farrakhan and his lieutenants' venomous diatribes against the Jewish people.

In a November 1993 speech, delivered at Kean College in New Jersey, Farrakhan's national spokesman, Khalid Abdul Muhammad, called Jews "bloodsuckers of the Black nation," acquitted the Nazis of responsibility for the Holocaust ("Don't nobody ever ask what the Jews did to Hitler?"), defamed the Pope as a "no good...cracker," and incited the murder of every white South African—"kill the blind, kill the crippled, kill the crazy," he said.

This is the same man who called Jewish Holocaust survivors "old, wrinkle-faced crackers."

Khalid's speech caused a firestorm and some serious repercussions for Farrakhan. He ceremonially "demoted" his young lieutenant for saying too much in the wrong place. Farrakhan would later say, however, "I had to rebuke him because I want him to be the great statesman he was born to be." Referring to Muhammad's "bloodsuckers" remark, he continued, "I didn't say it, Khalid did. Did he lie?" The audience at the University of Chicago roared back, "No!"

On February 19, 1994, in a speech in Baltimore, Khalid Abdul Muhammad cryptically articulated a chilling tirade that lays bare the very soul of the Nation of Islam.

I called them [Jews] bloodsuckers. I'm not going to change that…I am a truth terrorist. I am a knowledge gangster. I am a history Black hit man. You better watch out. [Praying] that God will kill my enemy and take him off the face of the planet, [he blasted] that old no-good Jew, that impostor Jew, that old hooknose, bagel-eating, lox-eating Johnny-come-lately perpetrating a fraud, just crawled out of the caves and hills of Europe, so-called damn Jew…I will never apologize to this bastard—never.[49]

He also blamed Jews for the crucifixion:

It was the white so-called Jews that set up a kangaroo court to charge Jesus with heresy and accepted a thief and robber named Barabbas over the good Black man Jesus, and under a system of capital punishment ordered the death penalty for Jesus, the Black revolutionary Messiah.[50]

The Cloak of Respectability

It seems that every extreme cult yearns, sooner or later, to gain a measure of establishment respectability. You will remember David Duke's abortive attempt to bring the Ku Klux Klan into the political mainstream. Farrakhan's dreams are running in the same direction.

Among the most obvious routes to respectability is being dignified through a presence on college and university platforms. Remember, it was at Kean College in New Jersey that Khalid Muhammad became a national figure. Unfortunately, it seems that the more radical the voices, the more the academic institutions clamber to give them a forum from which to spew their venom—all, of course, smugly defended by the "rights" of dissidents to enliven intellectual debate.

In September 1993, two months before Khalid's speech at Kean College, Farrakhan successfully pressured the Congressional Black Caucus to invite him to an African-American Town Meeting on Race, where Jesse Jackson and former NAACP Executive Director Benjamin F. Chavis embraced him. Congressman Kweisi Mfume declared "a sacred covenant" of political cooperation with the Nation of Islam. "No longer will we allow people to divide us," said Mfume (*Ministry of Lies*, p. 112).

The most visible attempt to credit the Nation of Islam has been crews patrolling public housing projects. Young Nation of Islam men, impeccable in their jackets, bright shirts, and bow ties, are seen by locals as saviors of their neighborhoods. Keeping drug dealers at bay, thus moving much of the criminal element out the neighborhood, certainly makes people sit up and take notice, especially in Washington and the secular media.

Farrakhan derives two gigantic benefits from the publicity. First, the Nation of Islam is doing something that works. When bullets stop flying through the windows, people tend to see those responsible as "good guys." It is not a matter of idealism; it is pragmatism. They do what others would not; therefore they must be all right.

Second, the street patrols provide great recruiting potential for the Nation of Islam, both in the neighborhoods and nationally, through favorable media reporting. Most people care little about the driving force behind the organization, much less the long-term consequences of being locked into the Farrakhan mentality.

Incidentally, the American Jewish Congress asked Labor Secretary Robert Reich to consider barring the Nation of Islam Security from receiving federal funds to patrol public housing projects because its sponsoring organization promotes bigotry, in violation of antibias laws

But, as with other hate groups, Americans may not listen until there is an exorbitant price to pay.

A few months ago I was at a clinic in Philadelphia undergoing a physical examination. One of the doctors was Jewish. During the course of the examination we began to talk about the situation in Israel and some of the things related to anti-Semitic outbursts in Europe and the United States.

"I'm 70 years of age," he said. "I can't remember saying what I'm going to tell you now to anyone in my life. But I will tell you that I'm afraid—afraid for what could happen to the Jewish people in this country."

While the extreme groups we have examined are still considered "fringe" elements, given the right circumstances, the doctor's fears may be well-founded.

9

Islamic Imperialism

On February 26, 1993, Americans were roughly shoved into a world we had hoped never to see close up: Terrorism had come to the United States.

As we sat transfixed before the evening news and watched images of black clouds billowing from the World Trade Center in New York City, the anguish etched on the darkened faces of people choking from smoke inhalation, and the stretchers bearing the dead and injured, we were suddenly aware that it could and did happen here.

For years, people in America had lived in mental isolation from the realities of bombs exploding among the innocent. Oh, we had seen it at a distance, but it wasn't the sort of thing we would expect to happen here in our own country.

Most of us, as we pass through those fleeting security checks and metal detectors on our way down airport concourses, never give much thought to why they are there.

The reason is that some people in the world are very upset with a situation in the Middle East that is to them intolerable. The State of Israel is a fact, and some people are ready and able to litter the face of the earth with death and debris in their quest to destroy it.

Names, places, and things that were once rather vague to us now begin to focus more clearly. Dead athletes at the Munich Olympics; blood-spattered airports in Athens, Rome, and Tel Aviv; the Achille Lauro; 241 bodies of young Marines in Beirut; Pan Am 103; Entebbe, Uganda; the Israeli Embassy and later the Jewish Cultural Center in Buenos Aires; the TWA pilot looking out from the small cockpit window with a gun at his head—perhaps they all seem a bit closer to home now. We have had our day at the World Trade Center and have been promised that there is more to come.

Why are there people so incensed with a country that has every biblical, moral, and historic right to exist that they are willing to kill others and themselves to reshape the map of the Middle East?

The fact that escapes most Americans (and unfortunately our leaders as well) is that the struggle has for all practical purposes little to do with politics. Nor does it have much to do with territory. It is not even, in the final analysis, an insoluble problem between Arabs and Jews. The overriding issue is a *religious* one, which is driven by radical elements that people in pluralistic religious societies in the Western world have great difficulty understanding. In the eyes of such radicals, it is a simple contest: Islam against the infidels.

Our media has fallen into the habit, by design or otherwise, of referring to Islamic radicals as fundamentalists. A friend in the Israeli Embassy in Washington D.C. had some words for me about the term.

"You should never," he said, "call them fundamentalists. This is not the truth. These people are radicals. When they are referred to as fundamentalists, the implication is that they are like fundamentalist Christians, and we know this is not the case."

Islam on the Rise

Until very recently Americans never gave the Muslim religion much thought. The reason was, of course, that Muslims were simply nowhere to be seen. As a matter of fact, back in 1934 there was only one Muslim mosque in the entire United States; it was located in Cedar Rapids, Iowa. Today Muslim mosques with their minarets are springing up all across the country. The current estimate of Muslims in the United States exceeds 4 million. It is a phenomenon being seen throughout the Western world.

France presently has a Muslim population of more than 2 1/2 million. England, where there were few mosques until recent years, now has a thousand or more, with the numbers of Muslims moving toward 2 million. The story in Germany is much the same. Islamic immigration has swelled their presence to an estimated 4 million.

Of a world population of more than 5 billion, Islam claims a billion followers of Allah and his prophet Muhammad. In other words, one out of every five people on the planet is claimed by Islam, and statisticians tell us that it is the fastest-growing religion in the world today.

Islam's rapid growth has set off warning signals among some observers in the Western world. Analysts project alarming growth figures for Islam by the year 2000. Muslims now make up approximately 19 percent of the world's population. By the year 2000, we are being told, the figure may swell to 35 percent. This will be due to the propensity of Muslims to have significantly larger families than either Christians or Jews.

Projected growth is also attributed to Islam's intense program of winning converts in the West. Libya and

Saudi Arabia invest heavily in such activities. The Libyan Institute for the Spreading of Islam has distributed 30 million copies of the Koran in translations for non-Muslims.

Saudi Arabia is turning Western petrodollars into mosques and missionary efforts. An obvious evidence of Saudi funding are the Islamic mosque and cultural center located ten minutes from the United Nations building in New York. The presence of this "world-class mosque," able to accommodate a thousand worshipers, is attributed by *Newsweek* to "the resurgence of Islamic power in the late 20th century" (*Newsweek*, March 9, 1992).

The Nature of Islam

Many of us have had the impression that Islam is the religion of the Arabs and have drawn certain conclusions based on this assumption. Although Islam did rise out of the Arabian desert in the seventh century A.D. and imposes Arabic cultural practices on its followers, most Muslims in the world are not Arabs.

Iran, for example, is not an Arab country. Iranians are Persians whose language is Farsi, not Arabic. Indonesia and Pakistan, with well over a hundred million Muslims each, are not Arab countries.

Furthermore, Muslims are not unified as a religion; they have sects as do Judaism and Christianity. The two most familiar are the Sunni and Shiite groups, which came into being after the death of Muhammad.

These facts are important when we consider that, although Muslims disagree on many things, often to the point of warring against one another, there is almost universal agreement on one subject: the existence of the State of Israel and a negative attitude toward the Jewish people. Another major point of conflict for mainstream Muslims is the Western "Christian" influence, which is viewed as a corrupting force in the Islamic world.

Opinions regarding the Muslim invasion of the Western world are varied. While many observers are deeply disturbed by the trend, some are much less worried. They reason that most Muslims are peace-loving people with no intention of becoming a disruptive force in Western society. Many Muslims, they believe, have come west because of oppression by their more radical Muslim brethren. And it is undoubtedly true, as with many Germans and Japanese in America during World War II, that some Muslims have been subjected to undue criticism over acts perpetrated by radical Islamic terrorists.

Another view is that Muslims coming west will be assimilated into the culture and eventually become more like their American and European neighbors than their Middle Eastern spiritual brethren. In the process, this line of reasoning goes, they will drop many Islamic practices that are abhorrent to Western ways of thinking. Such reasoning establishes a rationale upon which to reach a comfort level while facing a people and a system that may very well be a majority force in the future.

Before taking comfort in this line of reasoning, however, we should consider some basic facts about Islam.

Not a Pluralistic Religion

The fact that Islam is not a pluralistic religion escapes many people in America, where a religious "come one, come all" way of life has prevailed. Freedom of religion is not an inalienable right in the Islamic world, where conversion is strictly a one-way street.

When Jewish people see one of their number join another religion or cult, they may lament that person's decision. The same can be said of the Christian community. But for a Muslim, conversion to another faith can be an entirely different matter. Classic Islamic law allows non-Muslims to be converted *to* Islam but views conversion *from* Islam as a capital offense.

In America we consider Saudi Arabia a "moderate" Muslim country. But as our troops found during the Gulf War, Christian or Jewish religious expressions and symbols were taboo in public. There is no tolerance of church planters or synagogue builders in Saudi Arabia. In fact, religions other than Islam are outlawed there.

On September 3, 1992, a grisly execution was carried out at the marketplace in Qatif, Saudi Arabia. Pleas of innocence by Sadeq Malallah, 23, fell on deaf ears, and he was publicly beheaded for apostasy. The Saudi Interior Ministry issued a statement saying that Malallah was convicted of "insult[ing] God, the holy Koran, and Muhammad the prophet."

A Muslim-Christian Alliance

To assuage fears that where Islam reigns, one religion is supreme, Muslims have been proclaiming their commitment to pluralism. To prove their sincerity, they have gone so far as to promote a Muslim-Christian alliance.

A booklet produced by Muslims, however, exposes the underlying strategy. The booklet, *Muslim-Christian Alliance*, published in Istanbul, Turkey, contains revealing passages.

> Moreover, the saying of the Prophet Muhammad further states that in the end of time, true, pious, devout Christians will unite with Muslims and put a great fight together against the common threat of Atheism. For the time being, true devout Muslims must unite not only with their coreligionists, colleagues and fellow brothers, but with true Christian believers by skipping any dispute, since they have to unite urgently against the common enemy, aggressive, dreadful Atheism.[51]

When this objective is achieved, the booklet continues:

> Eventually, Christianity will be purified and get rid of all superstitions and misbeliefs and will unite with the true Islamic Religion, thereby Christianity will be in a way transformed into Islam, and by adopting guidance to Qur'an [Koran], the Christian community will become a follower of Islam and Islam Religion will be the leader position. The true religion of Islam will gain a great power as a result of that unification.[52]

The foregoing view expresses succinctly that where Islam becomes the majority, Jews and Christians are converted or relegated to inferior status.

No Division Between Secular and Sacred

The concept of the division between church and state does not exist in the world of Islam. One of the great conflicts currently being played out in the Middle East is between regimes viewed as "secular," such as was true in Iran before the fall of the Shah, and postrevolution Iran, which is ruled by religious clerics and Islamic law.

Author Robert Morey in his book *The Islamic Invasion* explains the Muslim attitude toward sacred-secular issues.

> To the Muslim there is no "secular" realm where he is free from Islam. To the devout Muslim, Islam is all of life....In Islam there is no "separation of mosque and state" that compares to the "separation of church and state" that prevails in most Western countries. Islamic religion and politics are one. As Egyptian-born Victor Khalil points out:

"Islam regulates every aspect of life, to the point that culture, religion, and politics in a Muslim country are practically inseparable."

Muhammad took the Arab culture around him, with all its secular and sacred customs, and made it into the religion of Islam.[53]

Holy War (Jihad) is Sanctioned

Slay the idolators [non-Muslims] wherever ye find them, and take them (captive), and besiege them, and prepare for them each ambush....Fight against such of those who have been given Scripture as believe not in Allah nor the Last Day....Go forth, light-armed and heavy-armed, and strive with your wealth and your lives in the way of Allah! (Sura 9:5,29,41).

For the devout Muslim, dying in a holy war for territory or the honor of Allah means an immediate entry into paradise. Therefore atrocities such as Iran's sending waves of children to certain death during its war with Iraq assured those children their place in heaven.

Wars against infidels (non-Muslims) are viewed as sacred ventures. For Islam the world is divided into two segments: the world of peace and the world of the sword. All that is Islamic is peace. All that is not waits to be conquered.

Thus all of Islam's wars of aggression against Israel were considered high priority campaigns for Allah and his followers. In their eyes, Israel occupies territory once held by Muslims, which is therefore sacred Muslim ground. Expelling the Jew is a matter of regaining the honor of Allah and reclaiming occupied Muslim land.

Why, during the Gulf War, did Sadaam Hussein lob scores of SCUD missiles at Israel while Israelis sat out the conflict? The premise is found in the principle of *Jihad*. To Sadaam's way of thinking, fellow Muslims would find it difficult to stand against the man who was punishing the Zionist infidels. In short, he was making Jihad against a common foe. However, he miscalculated his fellow Muslims' commitment to his holy cause. They were more interested in self-preservation than in Hussein's ruse to break the coalition against him.

We have considered only a few basic elements of the Islamic faith, enough to demonstrate the chasm-like gulfs between Judeo-Christian concepts and those of Islam.

The Islamic State

Perhaps the most frightening prospect facing the political world today is the specter of the radical Islamic state—a religious state that sees every objective in life directed toward making the Koran, as Muslims interpret it, the only way of life. Knives, bombs, guns, and bludgeoning instruments provide the means to drive infidels and dissidents into the light of Islamic law.

For Jews, Christians, and anyone else remotely interested in living under some semblance of democratic rule with inherent religious freedoms, the very existence of malevolent, Iranian-style states is an ominous threat. It is a threat that we can ill afford to ignore or to deal with responsibly. In the West, our affluence and self-preoccupation has tended to distract us from hearing or dealing with unpleasant matters. But radical Islam is not, as we might prefer to think, half a world away. It is in our midst, and Christians, Jews, and our way of life are in its gunsights.

Lest you feel these words are unduly reactionary, listen to a few of the proponents of a pure Islamic world speaking from their bases in America, as recorded in the PBS documentary *Jihad in America*, produced by Steven Emerson.

The only politics we understand is... shooting....The best thing is continued Jihad [holy war]. Nothing but Jihad. Even after the liberation of Afghanistan—the leaders have agreed to continue Jihad....Even after the Islamic government. They will not stop. They will go to Palestine...to liberate it. Anyone who stands in the way...we will smash him. Any ruler who will not let us go, we will go by force—Jihad.[54]

The Jihad, the fighting, is obligatory on you wherever you can perform it. Just as in America you must fast unless you are ill or on a voyage, so too must you wage Jihad. The word Jihad means fighting only—fighting with the sword.[55]

Allah's religion, be he praised, must offer scouts, must offer martyrs. Blood must flow. There must be widows. There must be orphans. Hands and limbs must be cut. And the limbs and blood must be spread everywhere in order that Allah's religion stand on its feet.[56]

The obligation of Allah is upon us to wage Jihad for the sake of Allah. It is one of the obligations which we must undoubtedly fulfill, and we conquer the lands of the infidels and spread Islam by calling the infidels to Allah. And if they stand in the way, then we wage Jihad.[57]

Then the sword is to absolutely be used and implemented, this is the principle.[58]

Jihad that has to be implemented. It is not a thing that we speak of. It is a thing that we do.[59]

Are these the rantings of members of the lunatic fringe? Or should we take these and their bedfellows at their word? For the answer, look east.

Israel

Terror groups such as Hamas and Islamic Jihad have committed themselves totally to killing Jews and destroying the peace process between Israel and the Palestinian people.

Their tools have been terrifyingly obvious: bombs strapped to bodies boarding buses and walking into intersections, ready to shred themselves and as many infidels as possible. We have seen it from a distance before. In World War II, fanatical Japanese suicide pilots flew bomb-laden planes into American ships. They did it for their emperor-god. Now, in the nineties, the kamikaze has returned—this time to the streets of Tel Aviv and Jerusalem.

Journalist Kenneth R. Timmerman interviewed leaders of Hamas, Islamic Jihad, and The Muslim Brotherhood in Damascus, Syria; Amman, Jordan; and Gaza, Israel. He discovered that the same forces that have driven anti-Semitism in Russia and Hitler's Europe and among today's neo-Nazis and their comrades are behind Islamic extremists. First and foremost is *The Protocols of the Elders of Zion.* Timmerman states:

> The belief in the *Protocols* is widespread not only among common people, but among the intelligentsia. Its ideas are deeply ingrained in the thinking of the radical Islamic groups opposed to peace with Israel. It colors the language they use and conditions their understanding of historic events, including the Holocaust and the creation of the State of Israel.[60]

183

Dr. Ahmad Bahar, a well-known spokesman of the political wing of Hamas, confirms Timmerman's observation.

> The *Protocols* were written by those who call themselves the Wise Zionists. The former leaders of Israel met together, and they planned how they would control the world. And they added to those plans the color of religion, in order to gather support from all the Jews from all over the world. In *The Protocols of Zion*, they claim that they are the masters of the world and the selected people of God, and they tried to implant those ideas and concepts into the minds of the Jews, as if it has been quoted directly by the Torah and the Talmud.[61]

In the minds of Hamas leaders such as Dr. Bahar, the Jews want to conquer the world; in that way they are doing the devil's work. "This is," he says, "the work of the devil, [and] why we are calling on the world to help us defeat the devil."

And why defeat the devil? It is not fundamentally a question of land, but one of the glory of Allah. Articles 7 and 8 of the Hamas *Covenant of the Islamic Resistance Movement—Palestine*, published in 1988, states the Islamic intentions and motivations clearly.

> Excerpt from Article 7: It looks forward to the fulfillment of Allah's promises in the not too-distant future. Allah's messenger [Muhammad] already spoke of a time when Muslims would fight the Jews and kill them— the Jew would hide behind rocks and trees. The rocks and trees say, "O Muslim, servant of Allah, this Jew is hiding behind me, come and kill him."

Article 8: Allah is the ultimate objective [of Hamas], His messenger [Muhammad] is its paragon, the Koran is its constitution, and *jihad* is its path, and death for the sake of Allah is its chief interest.

The Hamas Covenant speaks for itself. And the actions of its members write in blood—theirs and Israelis'—their commitment to their covenant.

At times the best way to get an idea of what is running through the bloodstream of fanatics is to read the graffiti and slogans they produce. Banners hung across the streets in Gaza say graphically what Islamic Jihad and their brothers in blood, Hamas, are thinking.

- The children of Israel will be sheep for the butchers of the Islamic Jihad
- The slaughter of the Jews is our choice to victory
- Yes to martyrdom
- Our dead are in heaven, while their dead are in hell
- We are seeking death, while the Jews seek life and its joys

Israel's Greatest Threat

The great nightmare for Israel, which lies beyond the illusive dream of peace with the Palestinians, is a Palestinian state. It is a given in the international community that Arafat and his PLO cohorts will ultimately have their ministate within the boundaries of Israel proper. The PLO's commandeering of the Orient House in Jerusalem as the future state's capital building says all that need be said. It gives the impression that even some Israeli leaders are resigned to what they believe to be the inevitable.

Such a state portends two serious problems—one lesser, the other much larger.

The first is Yasser Arafat's commitment to living in peace alongside the State of Israel. His sincerity has been, to say the least, suspect from the outset of the peace process. The PLO's failure to do what they promised in signing the peace accords is a tip-off. Arafat agreed to strike from the Palestinian Covenant the article calling for the destruction of Israel. He has not only neglected to do so but has in fact flatly refused to do so.

Throughout much of his terrorist career, Yasser Arafat has promised that if a Palestinian state were to become a reality, it would be only the first stage in the overall program to destroy Israel. This tactic of making peace when you are too weak to defeat your enemy is a staple in the Islamic system. Treaties mean nothing when Muslims become strong enough to defeat their foes. In this scenario, Islam always feels that time is on its side and that eventually infidel decadence will provide the right moment of opportunity to move against the infidels.

Arafat dropped a very broad hint that this might be his plan when, in Johannesburg, South Africa, he called on his Muslim brethren to join him in a Jihad to liberate Jerusalem from the Jews. His remarks were made long after the jubilant signing in Washington, in a place where the Chairman felt he was out of earshot of the media.

Many people in and out of Israel are beginning to wonder why Israel ever began talking with Arafat and the PLO. Perhaps a longtime friend and retired Israeli general said it best. After the signing ceremony in Washington, he confided, "We have just made a deal with the devil."

When I asked why Israel was pursuing such a course, he replied, "We had a choice: deal with a little devil, Arafat, or bigger devils still—Hamas and Islamic Jihad. We chose the little devil."

The general has a point, because a greater issue lies in the danger inherent in a "free election" process in the

Palestinian state. Incidentally, free elections are not relevant in the Muslim world. Should, however, Hamas and Islamic Jihad marshal enough forces to win a "free election," Israel and the West would assuredly begin to reap the whirlwind. Israel, through weariness with a perpetual state of war, and the West, by way of an astonishing political naiveté, will almost certainly find that they have sponsored a "peace" that will be too hot to handle.

For starters, the West, including some highly placed officials in Washington, have said they would welcome into the international community a Hamas-led government if its leaders would only back off from their terror tactics and come into power through free elections. But we must remember that these people and their companions in terror are committed wholly to the concept of killing Jews, destroying Israel, and subjugating the world—all in the name of Allah and Jihad. Therefore we are dealing with people who by their own admission cannot change their goals—only their tactics.

Should Hamas and Islamic Jihad prevail through such a process, two facts of life will emerge for Israel and the world at large. For Israel, it will mean living in a perpetual state of high military alert. These people make no bones about their intentions regarding Israel.

For the world, including the United States and Europe, the implications emanating from radical Muslims winning Islam's most hotly sought prize—a power and presence in Jerusalem—can only intensify the extremist Islamic crusade. If we are now witnessing what is being called by some the second great Muslim conquest, think of the Jihadian high that Muslim radicals would experience by successes they would interpret as winning the day in the Middle East. A radical Palestinian state could therefore become the ideological and inspirational launching pad for even more aggressive, global, Islamic imperialism.

Christians at Risk

Some people are convinced that if only Israel would acquiesce to the demands of the Palestinians, all our troubles with Islam would go away. Some even go so far as to implicate "Zionist" Israel as the real cause of the conflict in the Middle East—a Jewish presence, a global problem. That such is not the case is evidenced by the way Christians are being treated in those countries where militant Islamic groups are attempting to establish radical Muslim rule.

Egypt

The same radical forces that succeeded in assassinating Anwar Sadat for the crime of making peace with Israel are moving against Egypt's Christian population. Primary targets for the Muslim Brotherhood are Coptic Christians.

In May 1992 a group of 45 militants killed 15 people in the Egyptian village of Manshiet Nasser. Thirteen of them were Coptic Christians.

In the same village the Egyptian Organization for Human Rights reported that a militant Islamic group had prevented Christians from going to church and from gathering to worship in private houses. They had also beaten at least three Christians unconscious and murdered one of four Copts whom they had previously marked for execution. The militants forced Christian merchants to pay a special tax. To add insult to injury, they made them contribute to the construction of a mosque.

The Christians under attack—about 6 million of Egypt's 58 million people—are seen as pawns in a struggle for power. According to Hala Mustafa, an expert on Islamic politics, "The militants believe Christians stand between them and an Islamic state."

Hosni Mubarak, Sadat's successor, has been in the

same line of fire directed at the Coptic Christians. Again, the goal was to clear the way for an Iranian-style Islamic state.

Lebanon

Throughout its history Lebanon was among the few Middle Eastern countries resisting Muslim dominance. Before Syria's invasion and virtual annexation of Lebanon in the early eighties, the country was predominantly Maronite Christian. During the debilitating war that has devastated Lebanon, Syrian-backed Muslims openly boasted that they intended to eliminate the Christian infidel presence.

They meant exactly what they said. Thousand of Christians have been executed, mutilated, and driven from their homes. Again, this brutality is being done in the name of creating another pure Islamic state.

Dr. Walid Phares, professor of International Relations at Florida International University, leads the World Lebanese Organization. Dr. Phares and a coalition of Jewish and Christian organizations reject the Oslo Accords between the PLO and Israel. They instead favor comprehensive peace negotiations in which the Christian minorities in the region would be considered. Dr. Phares charges that the Middle East's 20 million Christians "have been subjected to gradual, systematic and multi-level ethnic cleansing." He makes a strong case for the protection of Lebanese Christians.

> The Arabization and Islamization of the country [Lebanon] is taking place at an increasing rate. The only part of the country that is not under this imposed oppression is South Lebanon, also known as the "Security Zone." If this zone is handed over to the

Beirut Government, this will mean the end of Lebanon as an independent nation and the final collapse of the Christians.[62]

Any Israeli-Syrian peace agreement will include Lebanon, which is controlled by Syria. A primary question will be the fate of the Southern Lebanese Christians should they suddenly find themselves under the control of the Syrians and their surrogates, the Hezbollah (Party of Allah). Should this happen, Hezbollah has made their intentions clear.

> In media broadcasts after one recent offensive, Hezbollah spokesmen warned Southern Lebanese Army members that they face death for collaborating with "the Zionist enemy." For its part Israel has set the dismantling of Hezbollah as a precondition to the reaching of a peace accord with Lebanon.[63]

Given the Arab track record for keeping peace agreements and the radical Hezbollah's Islamic plans for the region, there is little hope for Southern Lebanese Christians if they are left to the goodwill of those who seek to destroy them in the name of Allah.

Phares and others believe that a strong Israel is the best hedge against even more militant Muslim aggression toward the shrinking Christian population in the Middle East.

Sudan

The greatest tragedy associated with Islamic imperialism thus far has taken place in the Sudan. What has happened—although the secular media has been almost universally silent about it—is catastrophic in its scope.

On June 30, 1989, military officers under then Colonel Omar al Bashir took over the government through a coup and, in league with the National Islamic Front, intensified the program of Islamization that began in 1983.

With financial and military aid from Libya, Iraq, Iran, and other radical Islamic regimes, Bashir's government targeted Christians and animists for assimilation or annihilation in the quest for an Islamic state. Since the Islamization campaign began, Sudan's leadership has pursued Islam's policy of organizing the country by making Arabic the national language, Islam the national religion, and *Shari'a* (Islamic law) the national law. The chilling results are well-documented by the U. S. State Department, a host of human rights agencies, and other reliable individuals and organizations.

Middle East Concern identified the fundamental issues in conflict: "Jihad represents a collision of two cultures. Its aim is to supplant the indigenous Christian and animist religions (both predate Islam in the Sudan)." Their report quotes a reliable Christian commentator: "The current suffering will continue at the hands of this and future regimes until the south submits to Islam. There will be no peace otherwise."

The suffering referred to is severe, even when compared with the tragic situations witnessed in Bosnia and Somalia. Charred evidence of the Islamic crusade against Christians can be viewed in the villages and churches put to the torch by government troops.

The *Sudan Democratic Gazette* reports: "An authoritative study commissioned by the United States Committee for Refugees has revealed that 1.3 million Southern Sudanese have died since May 1983.... The report concludes that its estimate of 1.3 million deaths is conservative—as many as 2 million may have died." The *Gazette* further reports that 80 percent of Southern Sudan's 5 million population have been displaced since 1983. A U. S. State Department report issued in May 1993 states: "There are reports that thousands died of starvation in Meiram displaced camp last year, while local authorities would not release donated relief food." *Middle East Concern* asserts that non-Muslims must adopt Islam to qualify for food.

Among the most gruesome revelations of torture, systematic starvation, rapes, beatings, and assorted forms of brutality against Christians and other non-Muslims are summary crucifixions. Justification for these crucifixions is found in the Koran.

For those who resist Islam, *Sura* 5:33 says: "Their punishment is...execution, or crucifixion, or the cutting off of hands and feet from the opposite sides, or exile from the land."

Typical of these allegations is one by *Middle East Concern* that torture used against Nubian Christian leaders, especially pastors and evangelists, includes inverted crucifixion.

Jubilee Campaign, a human rights organization supported by 100 members of Parliament in Great Britain, leveled similar accusations. "In Sudan the civil war has led to a genocidal reign of terror directed against the Christian south by the Islamic regime in Kartoum with mounting evidence of the crucifixion of the male population of whole villages by government troops."

As is always the case, children in such tragic situations are not immune to the suffering. Starvation is inevitable. In the Sudan, slavery has also often been an alternative. Bishop Gassis of El Obeid alleges slave trading in Northern Sudan. "More than 20,000 Nuba Children," says the bishop, "have been sold with the fullest knowledge and connivance of the regime."

Such is the sordid record of Islamization in the Sudan, which is now busily exporting its Islamic brand of national purity. Sudanese Muslim radicals were named as suspects in the 1995 attempt to assassinate Egypt's Hosni Mubarak.

Algeria

The same possible scenario is a threat to non-Muslims in Algeria, where "infidels," particularly the French, who have vested interests there, are marked for assassination. The goal is to first purge the country of infidel elements and then Islamicize Algeria after the Iranian and Sudanese model.

In Algeria, 300 to 400 people have died each week in a savage war of attrition between the nation's rulers and Islamic insurgents. These anti-French Islamists are attempting to spread their radical message to the 4 million Muslims in France. Already their reign of terror bombings inside France has caught the eye of the international media.

According to allies of those attempting to forge an Islamic state in Algeria, this is only the beginning. In a 1992 interview in *Le Point*, the founder of Hezbollah confidently predicted: "In 20 years, France will become an Islamic Republic."

Israel

Christian Arabs in Israel are also very much at risk. Keep in mind that in the world of radicalized Islam, there are no benevolent regimes. Arabs of other persuasions are not granted immunity. It is a matter of record that more Palestinians died at the hands of their radical Muslim brethren during the Intifada in Israel than were killed by Israeli troops attempting to keep the peace.

During the negotiations for the Israeli withdrawal from a number of West Bank cities, some of the most urgent pleas for a continued Israeli presence were made by Christian Arabs. In Bethlehem, a Christian Arab town, many longtime residents sold their properties and left rather than face the future and the possibility of reprisals by Muslim extremists.

Islamic fanatics see the world of the infidel West much like dominoes tumbling before the irresistible force of Allah, the prophet, and their martyr-minded foot soldiers. As is typical in the West, many politicians, with economic interests dominating their thinking, are not taking the Islamic threat seriously or viewing it with any sense of urgency. Most American Christians are in much the same situation. They do not have the information, or they feel insulated by the "it can't happen here" fallacy. Perhaps Jewish people, given their history, are more alert to the danger. However, the reality is that all three—democratic governments, Christians, and Jews—are marked by those determined to conquer in the name of their god.

Let it be said unequivocally and for reemphasis: When it comes to Christians, Jews, and Muslims who disagree with the Muslim agenda, there are no benevolent radical Islamic regimes. We have seen the proof by looking at the real world as it exists in countries under relentless assault by Jihad-driven religious fanatics. Before it is too late, we had all better take a good look at what we see.

10

Moving into the Third Dimension

Israel's right to exist as a nation and combating anti-Semitism have been the solidifying ingredients in the evangelical-Jewish alliance since long before the rebirth of the modern State of Israel. The alliance between the Jewish people and Christians was sometimes so subtle in nature that many on both sides did not even recognize its existence. To those people, perhaps the content of this chapter has the look of something new—yet another new coalition or a resurgence or desire for ecumenical renewal.

Then again, there may be those who will feel that what we espouse is another wave in the rising tide in evangelical circles reflecting the "You're OK, I'm OK" theopsychology that has captivated some trendy evangelical thinkers. Theirs is becoming a movement essentially more horizontal than vertical in emphasis. By this I mean that the direction is being changed. Relationships between human beings and religious systems are supplanting what was once regarded as obligatory for evangelicals: that is making Christ known to all people everywhere.

I say with all kindness but with all clarity that the coalition under discussion here is not a replica of the recent evangelical/Catholic rapprochement declaration, *Evangelicals and Catholics Together: The Christian Mission in the Third Millennium,* which for all practical purposes implied that the Reformation was a mistake.

The coalition developing between an increasing number of conservative-minded Jews and like-minded evangelicals is different. The fact that evangelicals and Jews are standing together on issues of paramount importance to both groups and the United States is not a declaration of assimilation. Evangelicals are not promoting religious union with rabbinical Judaism; Jews are not publishing theses recanting objections to areas of Christian theology with which they have historically disagreed. No, this is a coalition growing out of the demand for a supportive relationship in America's *Second Revolutionary War*—one that is attempting to destroy the Judeo-Christian values and standards of morality upon which the nation was founded and has flourished.

Voices United for Israel, a group led by Esther H. Levens, is the convener of the National Unity Conference for Israel, a coalition of pro-Israel Jewish and Christian organizations numbering more than 160, with aggregate memberships of approximately 40 million people. Voices United for Israel has defined what a coalition is and has produced organizational guidelines accordingly.

"Coalition—An alliance, especially a temporary one, of people or factions, who come together for some specific purpose."

Following are some excerpts from the guidelines:

1. Coalitions are formed by the coming together of groups who share a common concern, although they may disagree on many other issues.
3. Since, by definition, coalitions are made up of groups and individuals who agree on some issues and disagree on others, each participant must decide which issues are essential to them.
4. Voices United for Israel is a coalition. Our mission is to build support for Israel, for the Jewish people, and for the fight against anti-Semitism.
7. Voices United for Israel makes no effort to control the agenda of its member organizations apart from this agreement.

These guidelines—typical of the documents of agreement being produced by like organizations—illustrate the strict division between an alliance relating to mutual concerns over relevant issues and one fostering ecumenicity.

We must remember that the first two dimensions in the Israel-Jew-evangelical relationship are mandated by the Word of God. Thus there is no question that Israel and the Jewish people find their most stalwart supporters in the evangelical community. Whatever else Jews may find with which to differ in conservative Christian theology, they cannot fault evangelicals for their convictions about Israel's inherent right to a homeland in the Middle East and their determination to stand against anti-Semitism in all its ugly manifestations. Historically, Christians with these commitments have remained firm in their stance toward Jews and Israel, in spite of the theological anti-Semitism common in the ranks of liberal religious elements professing Christianity.

Moving into a third dimension, which we shall consider in this chapter, is therefore a natural extension of this very strong alliance, which is already a fact.

It is refreshing to observe that after centuries of suspicion some Jewish people and evangelicals are making serious attempts to establish relationships in cultural and moral areas where both hold common interests. These ties are being established, not to see how much can be surrendered in the name of civility, but rather on the desire for an honest understanding of just who we are and what we are all about. Although with some members of both communities it is a fragile relationship, it is one better fostered than destroyed.

Religious Right: Threat or Ally?

Battle lines have been drawn between the now-entrenched secular hedonists of the sixties and those who hold to the traditional Judeo-Christian values and moral codes of the past. It seems so far behind us now—that era when right was right and wrong was wrong. I remember, as do many of you, that time with some measure of nostalgia.

The little town over in Michigan in which I grew up in the thirties and forties never would have qualified as a bastion of Christian normality. We had two churches in town, and one was liberal. Their specialty was sock hops for the kids and book reviews for the elderly. Those in the age groups somewhere in between didn't exude spiritual passion for either option.

The other church, although almost ultraconservative, was virtually invisible. It seemed to me as though they were sort of religious undercover agents. Their conversations with outsiders on spiritual matters were usually reserved for those who had made professions of Christianity or had joined the other church. The frowning counsel that people received from the members in such circumstances was usually confined to what they had done wrong.

Denizens of our town, with few exceptions, passed up

on the churches. Their commitment seemed to run more toward bars (we had three), bowling, and baseball.

We did not start our school days with prayer or a moment of nonsectarian silence; we did honor the flag by waking up the day with the Pledge of Allegiance. I remember that once the America Back to God quartet visited the school to sing, but that was about it.

Although it could be said that our community was functionally irreligious, it was totally observant when it came to the Judeo-Christian culture that was the norm for those decades. We all knew right from wrong, understood clearly what immoral acts were, and frowned on thieves, drunken carousers, and abusers of others. Furthermore, we maintained a sense of civic pride and humanitarian goodwill, and a measure of compassion for those in need. Romulus, Michigan, had been acclimatized by a culture that reflected, and in a way embodied, a Judeo-Christian way of life.

Unfortunately, that era has passed. Those in the political and cultural mainstream—those responsible for trashing the values—revel in having put a spin on the American culture that has sent it looping in the opposite direction from what America has always been. As a result the battle has been joined, and among the concerned few are evangelical Christians and Jewish people who have come together to say, "Enough is enough! This is the ground upon which we stand united."

The Religious Right and the Anti-Defamation League

In June 1994 the Anti-Defamation League published a 204-page study entitled *The Religious Right: The Assault on Tolerance and Pluralism in America*. The study was prepared, as stated by the ADL's David Cantor, to warn the country of the growth of an "exclusionist religious movement [the

Religious Right]" attempting to "unite its version of Christianity as a state power."

The study lambasted Christians of varying denominational persuasions, namely those in the Christian Coalition who are engaging in political activity. "The Religious Right," the ADL's study contends, "brings to cultural disagreements a rhetoric of fear, suspicion, even hatred." Religious Right activists were accused of showing contempt for the separation of church and state. "Fragile structures of consensus are bulldozed by sectarian, absolutist declarations. In this way, we proceed down the road to the 'Christian nation' trumpeted by these prophets of rage."

Pretty strong accusations. For lack of exposure to the material, most evangelicals who stood accused by the ADL did not realize they were being dragged into the court of public opinion.

When apprised of the situation and upon seeing certain groups on the list of credible "sources" assisting with the ADL's study—People for the American Way, Americans United for Separation of Church and State, and the homosexual group The Coalition for Human Dignity—evangelical leaders tended to shrug and say, "So what else is new?"

Intriguingly, those who returned fire at the ADL were not heavy-breathing, far-right fundamentalists. It was rather from within the Jewish community that significant numbers of riled voices were raised.

Jewish conservative columnist Don Feder had these words for the ADL:

> "The Religious Right: The Assault on Tolerance and Pluralism in America," a 204-page screed unleashed by the Anti-Defamation League last week, is an attempted political

assassination. The weapon, capable of putting a .44 caliber hole in any reputation, is inferences of anti-Semitism....The ADL is quite hysterical over the agenda of religious conservatives—opposition to gay rights, support for school prayer and the like. Instead of debating the issues like a gentleman, it stoops to implications of anti-Semitism to discredit a legitimate voice in the values debate....The ADL has betrayed its great mission in a political cause. The document it has fashioned discredits not the religious right but itself."[64]

Syndicated columnist Mona Charen, who is also a distinguished conservative panelist of CNN's *Crossfire*, wrote:

The Anti-Defamation League has committed defamation. There is no other conclusion to be reached after reading its new report....It is sad that an organization with a proud history of fairness should have descended to this kind of character assassination and name calling.... Anti-Jewish bigotry is far from the entire history of Christianity. Many Christians have been moved by their faith to help and protect Jews. Moreover, the history of Jews in the United States has been unprecedentedly benign. There have been isolated instances of violence against Jews—mostly perpetrated by the Ku Klux Klan. But those were rare exceptions. The serious Christians, as well as others, who have made America so hospitable deserve honor.

Finally, alas, there is a crude but undeniable fact that the ADL is in the anti-Semitism business. The more it finds, the greater its prominence, and the easier to raise money. It is playing upon the ancient fears and worries of American Jews—and is doing so dishonestly, with quotes out of context and flagrantly false accusations. It rails on imaginary enemies and betrays good friends.[65]

Midge Decter, a Distinguished Fellow at the Institute on Religion and Public Life, wrote in *Commentary Magazine*:

No doubt people hostile to the Jews exist here and there among conservative Christians. But so do people hostile to the Jews exist among liberal Christians and among the fiercest of secularists as well. The question, then, is why an organization long regarded as expert in the study of anti-Semitism should have singled out the conservative Christian for opprobrium—especially when, as a group, they have been perhaps the most outspoken friends of Israel in this country.

Judging from the book [ADL report] itself, the answer has to do not with Christians and Jews but with secular politics. The Religious Right is a force dedicated to implementing a series of ideas and measures that are anathema to most liberals. In attacking this agenda, and the people who support it as a threat to pluralism, the ADL has chosen to join hands with all those on the liberal Left who are determined to delegitimatize any challenge to the power they have long enjoyed over the basic institutions of American life and culture.

Thus has an organization which is devoted to fighting bigotry against Jews, and which now claims to be undertaking a defense of pluralism, defined the sensibilities and convictions of some 50 million Americans as beyond the pale. And thus has it become guilty of the one bigotry that seems to be acceptable these days—bigotry against conservative Christians. [66]

The most highly visible rebuttal to the ADL's study came in the Tuesday, August 2, 1994, edition of *The New York Times* in a large classified ad entitled "SHOULD JEWS FEAR THE 'CHRISTIAN RIGHT'?" The ad, produced by the conservative Jewish group Toward Tradition, carried signatures of endorsement from 75 prominent American Jews.

The response by this coalition of fair-minded, politically conservative Jews strikes at the heart of the issue by saying:

> The separation of church and state is not the same thing as the elimination of religious values and concepts from political discourse.
>
> Moreover, Judaism is not, as the ADL seems to suggest, coextensive with liberalism. Nor, we wish to emphasize, does the Jewish community speak in one voice on the religious and moral—and—political issues of our time.
>
> Above all, on the issue with which this community does speak with one voice, namely, the survival of Israel, the Jews have no more stalwart friends than evangelical Christians. Judaism teaches the principle of *Hakarat Hatov*, that we have a duty to acknowledge the good done to us. In issuing *The Religious Right* the ADL has among other things seriously violated that principle....

As a people whose history so vividly illustrates the bitter results of bigotry, we have a special obligation to guard against it, and all the more so when, as in the case of the ADL attack on our Christian fellow citizens, it emanates from within our own community.

The firestorm resulting from the response in *The New York Times* demonstrated two things. First, a deep division has developed in the Jewish community between traditional political liberals and the rapidly growing segment of Jewish people who are committing to a conservative position.

The attack from the ADL, and the response from Jewish conservatives, brought to light in a rather spectacular way the fact that there was now a positive third dimension in Jewish-evangelical relations.

There is also another factor to consider: The controversy clearly brought to the fore the fact that the central problem at issue was cultural and political; basically, it had little to do with religion. While there were at times attempts to throw tried and tested rhetorical grenades, such as "proselytizing" and "Christian anti-Semitism," into the arena, the real explosion was about the significantly increasing numbers of Jews who are opting to take the road previously less traveled—conservatism.

A View from the Right

There is a vast misperception in the Jewish community, and perhaps among some Christians as well, about what constitutes the Religious Right. On the one hand, there are those liberal, secular analysts—Jew and Gentile—who see in the Religious Right a cadre of theocratically crazed fanatics storming every sanctuary of American life in an all-or-nothing charge to rule or ruin.

On the other hand, there are evangelical Christians wondering why they are now listed as card-carrying members of the Religious Right. They are folks who never signed up but who are nevertheless counted. What's worse, they are being called by the current establishment "enemies of the culture—an ill-bred faction to keep an eye on."

Then there are uninformed Jewish people who are puzzled over just how dangerous the Religious Right is to their way of life. They are perhaps wondering if they should think more seriously about making *aliyah* to Israel.

What, after all, is the Religious Right? The Christian Coalition is often regarded and often referred to as being exclusively the Religious Right. It is as though the 1.7-million-member organization, with 1700 chapters across the United States and a budget of 25 million dollars, is all there is to the Christian Right. Perhaps this is due to the high profile of the group and their impressive list of successes in the political arena—successes which, by the way, have struck fear into the hearts of those who have brought the morals and mores of the sixties to downtown Washington D.C.

Even though the Coalition's 1.7 million members certainly has the ring of an impressive number and carries considerable clout at the polls, it by no means represents the whole of the evangelical conservative movement in America. According to a 1993 study by the City University of New York, Christian evangelicals make up 20 percent of the U. S. population—some 50 million people. Evangelicals are, as their immense numbers would indicate, a variegated tapestry of constituencies cut from a range of theological cloth.

What the Religious Right Is Not

There is a considerable amount of *straw manning* in the

case marshaled by liberals who are bludgeoning the Religious Right. That is to say, opponents are either misinformed as to the size, efficiency, and solidarity of the evangelical force, or they are creating a perception of strength to infuse fear into the populace, which will serve the liberal agenda. The facts are substantially different than the opponents of the Right wish to convey.

- **No leader, or group of leaders, mandates the way evangelicals vote**. Diversity of theological beliefs among those cast within the Religious Right is considerable and many times even politically contradictory. While some leaders certainly influence people who share their particular values and theological views, they by no means "control the vote." There is, for example, a sharp division of thought and practice regarding the Christian community's proper method of participation in political affairs. For this reason, until the present moral and spiritual crises stirred evangelicals to embrace political activism, Christians by and large united as denominational bodies to promote the faith, but they left the practice of politics to individual choice and conviction.

- **There is therefore no "united evangelical vote."** The facts will show that, like their less spiritually oriented fellow Americans, thousands of evangelicals are more inclined to vote pocketbook than principle.

- **Evangelicals are not committed to creating a theocratic political system that will force those with differing opinions to submit to authoritarian religious politicians.** Except for a tiny minority among Christians, conservatives hold that the only theocracy mankind will ever know will be realized when the Messiah returns to establish His kingdom.

While evangelicals believe in the principle articulated in Psalm 33:12, "Blessed is the nation whose God is the LORD," we fully recognize that there is a great difference between a nation that gives God His place and one that is a divine monarchy, as will be the Messiah's kingdom.

This is an extremely important point because the focus of the attack against the Religious Right is their intention to destroy pluralism in America. This was the central theme of the ADL study. But that is not the case; very few evangelicals oppose pluralism. Therefore the objections of the ADL and their friends to Christian political activism evaporate.

If we are looking for someone seriously bent on taking away America's religious pluralism, we had better go to the radical Islamic elements that have been exposed in previous chapters. They will be glad to clarify their intentions.

Panic on the Left

It is true that a few people cast with the Religious Right have made strong and rather bizarre statements about putting God on the throne in America. Such declarations of intent are for the most part taken out of context and are used to scare the wits out of people like those in the Jewish community. Or, if spoken with the actual intent to call for a Christian theocratic system, as a few voices do, they do not represent the views of any significant element in evangelicalism. These are facts that I believe are very well known to those on the left side of the political spectrum currently feigning hysteria.

Such proponents of what has been dubbed the Religious Left are understandably shaken by growing and substantial resistance to the radical social agenda they have brought into the mainstream of American life.

These social reconstructionists have been riled by the increasing visibility of informed Christians who are becoming involved in the political process because they want to do something that will put the brakes on the runaway hedonism espoused by their critics. (Incidentally, becoming involved in the political process is precisely what national leaders have urged responsible citizens to do since the republic was founded.)

Christians are now in the political arena in an effort to redirect the reverse culture spin that is forcing radical anti-Judeo-Christian patterns on them, their families, and life in their communities. Thus to imply as is being done that various groups with Judeo-Christian moral and spiritual convictions are devious and dangerous for such acts as informing constituents about the voting records of public officials on issues of mutual concern is beyond the pale of serious argument.

Virtually every negative political campaign ad spun by local, state, and national candidates from both parties features the "shabby" voting record of the opponent. Also, the track records of the self-appointed critics of the Religious Right are in themselves enough to discredit their objections.

The truth is that the panic on the left is a self-created phenomenon. The growing perception of massive numbers of Christians uniting to express outrage and promote a return to decent standards of conduct within the nation is the direct result of the relentless onslaught by those who are now loudly complaining about mortal danger from the Religious Right.

Growing from the Roots

What we are witnessing today is a spontaneous growth from the grassroots that exceeds any single or multiple segment of the Religious Right. The motivation for the great coming together of evangelicals and others is not a partisan political whim. No, it is millions of people who are beginning to react to the systematic gutting of the values upon which this nation was built. They are rebelling against the raucous repudiation of Judeo-Christian standards and values by people who revel in the radical.

Having rejected divine standards of belief and conduct, the new-wave humanists who are now in the mainstream are groping to establish a God-free system that will somehow pass for organized society—a sort of compass-less commitment to something no one is quite sure of. The "new morality" of a few years ago has become the "no morality" of the nineties. The process of realigning America, in view of the religious left, is now in the regimentation stage, and the proponents of the new wave have little time or tolerance for those steered by divine absolutes.

The perception of increased political clout by the Religious Right is enhanced by increasing numbers of Americans who are by no stretch of the imagination evangelicals—for example, politically conservative Jews—expressing their displeasure with the odious erosion of Judeo-Christian culture. These Jewish people recognize, as do persecuted Christians in other countries, the implied peril at hand when religious minorities are singled out as dangerous subversives.

Here lies a serious potential problem. If, in order to gain short-term political advantage, critics can depict the Religious Right as a malicious body of fanatics controlled by a few kook-fringe malcontents, the residual impact could be devastating. The vast majority of people identified with the Religious Right are serious-minded citizens who reflect the majority opinion of Americans on fundamental questions of decency and morality.

The Third Dimension

America has been very good to the Jew—and to the

rest of us, for that matter. Remember columnist Mona Charen's comment: "Moreover, the history of Jews in the United States has been unprecedentedly benign...the serious Christians, as well as others, who have made America so hospitable deserve honor."

Mona Charen's point is well–taken, and it answers effectively those in the ADL and others, including mainstream Protestant liberals, who are crying wolf about the current return to conservative values. Their objection, of course, is motivated by a distressing sense that the liberalism they so cherish is losing the day. It is, frankly, more than they can bear.

But the reality is that Jews, in coming to America, found something different—far different from what they left in pogrom-blighted Europe. They had entered a young nation, as yet not completely jaded morally or spiritually. The culture in the United States was firmly Judeo-Christian, and even though people had their differences, a Jew could feel comfortable among Christians who took their religion more or less seriously.

Rabbi James A. Rudin, of the national staff of the American Jewish Committee, said: "America *has* lost its moral compass. It seems adrift. But we have an obligation as Jews to ask: Where will it point?" America has "never been a secular country, and it never will be." Religious beliefs have "always shaped the public dialogue."

"But my concern with the religious right is," Rudin continues, "Do they want to change the rules of engagement? It's a very important question. What kind of America will it be" if the Christian right takes charge?

I can't speak for all my evangelical peers, but I think I can answer the rabbi's question, which is legitimate. The kind of America that conservative Christians want is an America centered again in what we have lost.

Herbert Zweibon, Jewish founder of Americans for a Safe Israel, believes "that Christian conservatives have a right to be concerned about the moral and social direction of the country and have the right to express themselves."

"Does this," he reasons, "in any way defame the Jewish community? Not at all. Conservative Christians and Orthodox Jews share the same beliefs on many social and moral issues" (Rod Dreher, *The Washington Times*, June 28, 1994).

Herb Zweibon obviously believes the Religious Right's "rules of engagement" are fundamentally programmed in the right direction.

Jewish conservative columnist Don Feder, in his book *Pagan America*, is seeing, as a Jew, exactly what concerns the evangelicals about whom Rabbi Rudin wonders and worries. In the introduction to his book Feder writes:

> By *Pagan America*, I mean that this is no longer a Judeo-Christian nation, animated by the ethical vision of the Bible, with its special emphasis on honesty, hard work, caring, and self-discipline. Instead, we are evolving into a type of Canaanite culture (unrestrained hedonism, ritual prostitution, child sacrifice and the civic virtue of Sodom) which my ancestors encountered at the dawn of moral history.

Actually, what concerned Christians are seeking is nothing new. It is a return to the Judeo-Christian standards upon which the United States was built. The real struggle is between proponents of radical liberal ways of life, as opposed to those holding traditional conservative ways of life. It is a clash of cultures. This is precisely why conservative Jews and evangelicals are finding a new dimension in their relationship. Viewed in the light of Judaism's traditional teachings, there is much more for Jews to cheer than to fear in the reassertion of conservative values.

Columnist Don Feder says:

My conservatism is God-centered, premised on a passion to nurture the best in human nature, which flows from our acceptance of divine injunctions. It is based on a worldview of the patriarchs and prophets, grounded in the heritage of the people who first taught humanity to think in moral terms.

I want Christians to know that there are Jews (not Jews by birth, but Jews by conviction) who are every bit as anguished as they over the moral decline of this nation.[67]

Support for abortion on demand, legitimatizing homosexuality, and banishing religion from the public sphere is the very antithesis of normative Judaism....

Jewish liberalism can only be explained as a matter of blind faith. Liberalism is the secular creed of the non-religious.[68]

Jewish commentator Dennis Prager, in his newsletter *Ultimate Issues*, confronts the question of homosexuality and family values.

Prager begins by noting that Judaism alone among the religions of the ancient world opposed homosexuality.

In Greece and Rome, among Phoenicians and Canaanites, a man's preference for other men, or boys, was of no more consequence than another's choice of beef over mutton.

Judaism was the first religion to insist that sex be confined to marital relations....

Prager observes that Judaism started a moral revolution, later carried forward by Christianity, in demanding that sex be sanctified, raised from the animal to the spiritual plane....

> By insisting that romantic love could be
> found only in marriage, it began the process of
> raising the status of woman from breeding
> animal to fully human.[69]

These observations by Feder and Prager, two of the leading media spokesmen for conservative Jewish concerns, emphasize the fact that the cultural warfare in which we are now engaged has nothing to do with Jews against Christian values by virtue of their being Jews. Jewish people opposing the quest to return to traditional American values are simply joining their secular-humanist Gentile bedfellows in reshaping the cultural environment.

Don Feder is quite correct when he says that Jewish liberalism is "a matter of blind faith...the secular creed of the non-religious." The same can be said of Christian liberalism. They have left the faith to create another form of religion. As at the Tower of Babel, it is conceived in the mind of man, produced by human ingenuity, and built by their own hands.

Evangelical Christians and Orthodox Jews have a name for it—apostasy.

For this reason, it is not surprising to witness the fusion of thinking and cooperation between conservative Jews and evangelicals when it comes to matters related to morality and values. It is only the natural outgrowth of adherence to Judeo-Christian traditions.

The Real Irony

The ironic thing in the controversy between the Religious Right and segments of the Jewish community is that, by and large, it is not devoutly religious Jews who have taken umbrage at what is being attempted by their contemporary Christian counterparts. It is the *nonreligious* segment of the Jewish community that trumpets their sensitivities about conservative gains, which they claim offend their Judaism and portend the grave danger of a Christian moral takeover.

I might add that these liberals are using code words and phrases—such as "proselytize," "prophets of rage," "paranoia," religious "hysteria," "exclusionist religious movement," and the like—in precisely the same way enemies of Jews have persistently done while engaging in classic "Jew-baiting." But this time the shoe is on the other foot. "Christian-baiting" is a page out of an old book, and perceptive Jews know the story line very well indeed.

William J. Bennett, former U.S. Secretary of Education and codirector of Empower America, buttresses the point.

> Our political culture has sunk to the point where people who have time-honored religious beliefs that inform their politics now become the object of scorn and ridicule. On the issues, "the religious right" now stand where most Americans stood 30 years ago. The irony is that the critics of the "Christian right" are often guilty of the things they protest to be offended by: intolerance, mean-spiritedness, divisiveness and even bigotry.[70]

Rabbi Daniel Lapin, founder of Toward Tradition, believes "that the old-line liberal Jewish groups [like those cited above] are becoming irrelevant or even counterproductive to meeting the new, increasingly conservative and religious interests of American Jews" (*Human Events*, October 28, 1994).

In calling for a strong alliance with the Christian Right, Rabbi Lapin declares: "Right now, we are facing a vicious and cruel society terrorized by predators....Jews in particular don't do well in civic anarchy; Jews could be very well the first to suffer under these conditions."

He added, "We have a tough choice, I will concede. We can continue with our secular society entirely stripped of faith or move toward a benign society that has returned to the Christian faith....We can only thrive under the conditions of law and order and we are here to affirm that our allies in returning America to these conditions are [Christian conservatives]" (*Human Events*, p. 5).

A kind of summary statement of what this is really all about is found in an article by Michael Ledeen, "Should Jews Fear the Religious Right?" published in October 1994 by *Moment Magazine*. Ledeen writes:

> This brings me to the question of the proper relationship between American Jews and conservative Evangelical Christians. I believe it is no accident that Evangelical Christians have been among the strongest supporters of Israel....It is also no accident that...Christian Evangelicals believe Jews are a special people, uniquely worthy of love and support. That there is an intense ambivalence between us is as old as Christianity—for believing Christians, our failure to convert to Christianity is, to put it mildly, perplexing—but there is a lot of affection, and many areas in which we should be delighted to have their support, and give ours to them. When we differ with them, the tone of our criticism should be sadness, not virulent, blanket condemnation of the sort heard from Clinton, the Democrats and the ADL.[71]

Facing the Gathering Storm

We have clearly moved into a culturally contentious period when those who share Judeo-Christian values are becoming more conspicuous and less appreciated. It is therefore not surprising that we are now witnessing manifestations that should arrest our attention and provoke serious thought. In spite of all sane reasons to the contrary, anti-Semitism is a persistent problem in the Western world. Here in America we see some distressing attitudes rising.

At the same time, the kind of Christians—and their virtues—that played such a large role in making this country what it is are being singled out as misfits by militants with self-serving agendas.

I don't believe these are unrelated facts of life. I believe these realities should bring evangelicals and Jews closer together, not drive them apart.

When all is said and done, this alliance between Bible-believing evangelicals and Bible-believing Jews is not like any other that comes to mind. Ours is, to employ an overused word, unique. Other alliances can easily fall victim to stress of one kind or another and be dissolved. Each side can go the way that seems most appropriate to its vested interests. That is not true at this juncture for evangelicals and Jews. We are inexorably bound by Judeo-Christian principles, moral conviction, and, in significant areas, biblical mandates.

To flee these principles under the tyranny of a culture gone mad is to lose everything—the country, of course, suffering the greatest loss. On the other hand, refusing to bend will assuredly bring a return to some of the old ways of intimidation—and perhaps even liquidation—that history has so much to tell us about.

What I'm saying is this: Entering this third dimension, given biblical prophecy of the end times, was inevitable. Whether some people find certain areas of disagreement within the alliance is not the primary issue. As time goes on we will find that we cannot turn from one another and opt for a way out. Jews and Christians of conviction have been duly identified and marked—as surely as Jews have worn identifying badges through lamentable situations across the centuries. Each of us must realize that now there is no turning back. We must stand together or else be spiritually and morally liquidated.

11

Bridges

Christians who feel a sense of appreciation for Israel and wish to achieve a positive relationship with the Jewish community often ask how to go about it. I have some suggestions.

Go to Israel

This may seem like a rather costly first step, but I can tell you from personal experience how much it can mean. I visited Israel for the first time in 1970. That trip revolutionized my outlook on many things.

First, for those who are serious about the Bible, the Scriptures will come alive in an entirely new way. Geography, distances between cities, and many subjects studied for years but never quite focused in your thinking will be clarified.

Meeting Israelis and being personally *up close* to the

phenomenon the Jewish people call "the ingathering of the exiles" is a moving and perspective-altering experience. Jews have returned to Israel from more than a hundred countries. When people see the masses of Russian Jews who have been part of the great Russian exodus, studying the return of the Jews to their homeland in the last days becomes an exciting enterprise.

Then there is the matter of experiencing life in the Middle East. We read and see reports from that troubled part of the world through the editorial rooms of the secular media. Being in Israel and seeing life as it really is will give you much better discernment about events in Israel and the Middle East.

For example, a short visit to the Golan Heights will demonstrate immediately how important that piece of real estate is to the security of the nation and why there has been so much controversy over its return to Syria.

Of particular help is seeing firsthand the prophetically related elements now developing in Israel. I strongly recommend that people take such a journey with a group or a person capable of communicating competently in the area of prophecy. I would further recommend traveling, while in the country, with a Jewish tour agency. Christians will want to interact with the Jewish community in Israel and study issues from the Israeli perspective.

Don't make price the primary factor in planning your trip. While few people have extra dollars to toss about, remember that for most people this is a once-in-a-lifetime trip. It is worth the investment to make sure you are exposed to as many aspects of Israel as possible. Very low tour fares, cut-rate hotels, and expensive side trips to important places not included in the regular price of the tour can add up to a bad experience.

All in all, a tour to the land so close to the heart of God and true believers can put a new face on your prayers for the peace of Jerusalem.

Visit Your Local Synagogue

This is something you can do much closer to home and of course with much less expense. Rabbis and synagogue or temple members as a rule welcome visitors to their Friday evening Shabbat services. I suggest that you call the synagogue, tell them you would like to visit, and ask about the time of the service.

Let me share with you how effective this can be in building bridges of communication with the Jewish community in your area.

While pastoring the Timberlake Baptist Church in Lynchburg, Virginia, I had a true lover of Israel and the Jewish people as a member of the congregation. His name was Gordon Ingham, and in many respects he became a spiritual father to me.

Gordon was a faithful deacon of the church and active in the ministry of the Gideons. He was also a straightforward witness to his faith. The great loves of his life were Scripture distribution, the Jewish people, and Israel. The Agudath Sholom Synagogue rarely sponsored a bazaar or public event that Gordon did not attend.

When an article or editorial appeared that was negative toward Israel, within a few days Gordon would have a response in the "Letters to the Editor" section of the paper. Being English, he had lived through the years of the British mandate, had seen the deterioration of Britain's support for Israel, and was deeply concerned that the same would not be the case in U.S.-Israeli relations.

Gordon never allowed our church family to forget their obligation to "pray for the peace of Jerusalem" and stand by Israel and the Jewish people. It would not be far off the mark, in the most constructive possible way, to say that Gordon was Israel's ambassador in Timberlake Baptist Church and the evangelical Christian community.

It would also be fair to say that he represented the evangelical community among the Jewish people in Lynchburg and the Commonwealth of Virginia.

Upon his death a rather remarkable thing occurred. I conducted his memorial service, and when I looked out on the auditorium I saw the president of the synagogue and other members of the Agudath Sholom congregation. Frankly, I had expected members of the Jewish community to be in attendance. Following the service, they came with tears to express their deep sense of loss at the departure of such a warm friend of the Jewish people.

Then the president made a request: "Would you be kind enough to attend the service at the synagogue next Friday evening?"

When I arrived, I was informed that the major portion of the service that evening would be devoted to a eulogy for Gordon Ingham. I must confess that it was one of the most moving experiences of my tenure of ministry in Lynchburg.

Among other things said that evening was a tribute I feel all evangelical Christians should strive to have said of them, even if they never hear it while alive.

"Gordon Ingham," the speaker said, "was a man who represented the best of everything in Christianity."

Later a plaque was placed in the synagogue in memory of this man revered as a Righteous Gentile.

Gordon's genius? There was none. He was simply willing to show himself friendly and stand up to be counted.

You can do the same.

Visit a Holocaust Center

I described earlier in this book the profound impact I experienced when visiting Yad Vashem in Jerusalem. Most of my readers may never have that opportunity, but there are a number of Holocaust memorials across the United States that you can visit.

I urge every visitor to Washington D.C. to make a stop at the United States Holocaust Memorial Museum. In very graphic ways it refutes the revisionist folly purporting that the Holocaust never occurred. It will allow you to look into the heart of the Jewish people and acquire a new sense of appreciation for Jewish attitudes about the Holocaust.

Taking a group from your church and youth group to a memorial in your area can be very helpful for Christians not well-acquainted with the world of the Jew. At the memorial in Washington there is an excellent exhibit for children.

To assist you, we have listed some of the larger Holocaust centers in an appendix at the end of this volume.

Sponsor a Thank God for Israel Day in Your Church

This is not a daunting project. It does take planning and preparation, but it will be well worth it. Do you remember my report on the Boca Raton Bible Church Thank God for Israel Day?

I have been involved in or have been informed of scores of such events over the course of several years now, and I must say that I have never heard a negative report about them. They always seem to improve relations between evangelical churches and their Jewish neighbors.

If you would like to sponsor such an event, contact a church that has done it, or get in touch with a group such as The Friends of Israel, who can assist you.

Do Something Tangible to Show Your Solidarity

The organization with which I currently serve has a

grove in the Menachem Forest in Jerusalem where, during each of our two annual tours to Israel, we stop to plant trees. Thousands have been planted by tour guests or on behalf of those who wish to have a tree planted in memory of a friend or loved one in the Friends of Israel Grove.

This may appear to be a small thing, but it seems to have a very positive impact on participants. There is also the satisfaction of, in cooperation with the Jewish National Fund, having a part in the reforestation of Israel.

Many thousands of evangelical Christians have contributed to Jewish agencies involved in the emigration of Jews from the former Soviet Union. One Jewish organization alone has received more than a million dollars in contributions from Christians who are concerned about the future of Jewry in the Commonwealth of Independent States countries. Various Christian agencies are also vitally involved in the effort. The important thing is to express in a tangible way your desire to have a part in the lives of Russian Jews at a time of critical need, and in the process demonstrate to the Jewish people that you are willing to do more than just talk about your love for Israel.

Other projects, in a great variety of situations, are the types of programs Christians can feel comfortable in supporting.

Words from Jewish People Who Have Interrelated with Evangelical Christians

I asked some people who are prominent in Jewish organizations if they would be kind enough to relate their personal experiences and give suggestions for other Jewish people who might have questions about establishing relationships with evangelicals. What follows is a summary of their quotes on a variety of subjects.

Personal Observations

When I speak to Jewish groups, I encourage them to get to know Christians personally. I tell them that there is a broad array of Christians and as many differences among Christians as among Jews.

A classic Jewish story illustrating this is about two men who were found after years of being stranded on a deserted island. Before they left, they insisted that they show their rescuers what they had constructed during their years of isolation. They showed them a building where they ate dinner. Another building was where they slept at night and entertained each other. Then they came to three distinctive-looking structures that evoked a question from the rescuers.

"What are these three buildings?" they asked.

"This is where I go to synagogue," the first said.

Pointing to another of the buildings, the second man said, "That is where I go to synagogue."

"But what is the third building for?" asked an inquisitive rescuer.

"Ach! That is the synagogue neither of us would ever set a foot in."

The point of the story, of course, is that Jewish people and Christians may well have much more in common than they think.

My own personal relationship with Christians goes back to my early childhood. Growing up in Kansas City, the majority of my friends were Christians....As a senior in high school, I was elected president of the National Council of Christians and Jews....It took me awhile to differentiate between Catholics and Christians and other Christians. I have only begun to recognize some differences between what would be called "Mainstream Protestants" and other Christians.

My overwhelming experience with Christians has been a positive one. There is oftentimes a great sense of calm and peace that people who have accepted Christ seem to exhibit. Contrary to the demonization that some liberal Jewish organizations are attempting to do, most of the Christians whom I have met are kind and gentle people. Many are doing extraordinarily wonderful things for both the Jewish people as well as others.

I have found that mutual respect and mutual trust are built upon an open and honest exchange. Most people do not want to offend other people. This is true of both Jews and Christians. Many Christians are unaware when they say things that sound harsh to Jewish ears. A classic is, "Many of my best friends are Jewish." Interaction with Christians allows both of us to delete from our language words that are offensive to each other.

I personally became aware that we Jewish people had dear, loyal friends in the Christian community as a college student 20 years ago. As an adult working closely with Soviet Jewry for the past ten years, I found, even before the gates of emigration were opened, that there were Christian friends pleading the *refusenicks'* cause in the churches and in our nation's capital.

I believe that it is important for Jews to learn that when a Christian has a genuine interest in you as a person that he often, from his faith, wants you to convert or be baptized so you will be with him in the afterlife. This is born out of a genuine affection and, when taken as such, should not be offensive. Some Jews resist such efforts, however, and feel threatened as they recall age-old times of forced conversions.

In 1992 I worked with the Israeli Likud Party to deliver our messages to churches. I was treated with utmost respect in every church and Christian organization I visited. I found that evangelicals care and stand with us for Israel's continued prosperity and the fight against anti-Semitism.

Common Ground

It is the Judeo-Christian heritage (belief in one God, the Bible, the Decalogue, the sanctity of human life, and the centrality of the family) that forms the basis for interaction and collaboration between evangelicals and Jews. These beliefs also formed the basis upon which our Founding Fathers created the Declaration of Independence and the Constitution.

Similarly, our jointly held beliefs formed the basis for the establishment of the State of Israel. Its existence as the expression of G-d's covenant with the Jewish people is essential for both believing Christians and Jews.

As a conservative Jew who believes in the validity of the Holy Scriptures and G-d's promises to the Jewish people, I feel we have common ground with Bible-believing Christians who fully recognize these promises as well.

I firmly believe that we have a set of common values that derived from Mount Sinai, and those values are the guides for individuals and societies to lead a decent and orderly life. These common values have caused those who want to have power over other human beings to view us as enemies.

Let's not forget that when Sadaam Hussein invaded Kuwait and shortly thereafter the Temple Mount riot occurred, the world overwhelmingly turned its back on Israel. It was in that time of crisis the evangelicals who defended Israel, and many pastors were pleading the case for supporting Israel from their pulpits.

Standing Together

We must acknowledge, accept, and respect differences among Jews and Christians but never let these distinctions overshadow the overwhelming important issues we have in common.

We must talk...between our two peoples, whether we view each other as friends or enemies. World Jewry shudders when Israel is treated unfairly by media bias. It is important for Jews to be reminded that evangelical Christians are often portrayed by the media in the same fashion.

By creating an open dialogue between us, we can become educated on precisely what we do agree upon and create a solid base from which constructive work can be done.

It is important for Jews to express their appreciation for Christians' help in the fight against anti-Semitism and for the State of Israel. It is important for Jews to point out that Christians also benefit by fighting anti-Semitism.

So I would advise my fellow Jews to look to the areas of agreement with the evangelicals on issues of public policy; to join with them on positions that emanate from our common beliefs. And there are many. Both groups believe in and foster personal responsibility, a code of ethics, strong family life, law and order. That there are areas of disagreement is secondary...surely there are many...issues upon which there would not be complete agreement. But those differences are between allies, to be resolved by discerning the will of G-d.

On the question of Israel, I would say to my coreligionists that the evangelicals are not only the best friends we have, but in large measure the only friends we have. The bottom line is, as I see it, that for America, we should join the evangelicals as fellow Americans; for Israel, we should join with evangelicals as fellow servants of G-d.

And so, we see that both Jewish people and evangelical Christians have a desire to build bridges of understanding and appreciation for one another. Let us not continue to make it a difficult endeavor. Furthermore, may we as individuals determine to make the first move toward recognition and solidarity.

Appendix

Learn More About It

To enhance your understanding of the Holocaust, following is an alphabetical list of Holocaust museums, memorials, libraries, resource centers, and more in the United States and worldwide. If there is a facility near you, I encourage you to visit it.

Allentown Jewish Archives
Holocaust Resource Center
702 North 22nd Street
Allentown, PA 18104

Anne Frank Center, USA
584 Broadway, Suite 408
New York, NY 10003

Auschwitz Study
Foundation, Inc.
P. O. Box 2232
Huntington Beach, CA 92647

Babi Yar Memorial Fund
7 Nemanskaya Street
252103, Kiev 103, Ukraine

Beit Lohamei Haghetaot
Kibbutz Lochamei-Haghataot
D. N. Oshrat
25220 Israel

Center for Holocaust Studies
Brookdale Community College
765 Newman Springs Road
Lincroft, NJ 07738

The Dallas Memorial Center
for Holocaust Studies
7900 Northaven Road
Dallas, TX 75230

Dayton Holocaust Resource Center
100 East Woodbury Drive
Dayton, OH 45415

El Paso Holocaust
Museum and Study Center
405 Wallenberg Drive
El Paso, TX 79912

Fortunoff Video Archive
for Holocaust Testimonies
Sterling Memorial Library
Room 331-C
Yale University
New Haven, CT 06520

Holocaust Awareness Museum
Gratz College
Old York Road & Melrose Avenue
Melrose Park, PA 19126

Holocaust Center of
The North Shore Jewish
Federation
McCarthy School
70 Lake Street, Room 108
Peabody, MA 01960

The Holocaust Center of
Northern California
639 14th Avenue
San Francisco, CA 94118

Holocaust Education and
Memorial Centre of Toronto
4600 Bathurst Street
Willowdale, Ontario
Canada M2R 3V2

Holocaust Education
Center and Memorial
Museum of Houston
2425 Fountainview Drive, Suite 270
Houston, TX 77057

Holocaust/Genocide Studies Center
Plainview/Old Bethpage
John F. Kennedy High School
50 Kennedy Drive
Plainview, NY 11803

Holocaust Learning Center
David Posnack Jewish Center
5850 South Pine Island Road
Davie, FL 33328

Holocaust Memorial
Foundation of Illinois
4255 West Main Street
Skokie, IL 60076

Holocaust Memorial
Resource and Education
Center of Central Florida
851 North Maitland Avenue
Maitland, FL 32751

Holocaust Research and
Education Center of Moscow
Bulatnikovsky pr. 14-4-77
Moscow 113403, Russia

Holocaust Resource
Center and Archives Queensborough
Community College
222-05 56th Avenue
Bayside, NY 11364

Holocaust Resource
Center of Kean College
Thompson Library, Second Floor
Kean College
Union, NJ 07083

Holocaust Resource Center
Keene State College
Mason Library
Box 3201, 229 Main Street
Keene, NH 03431

Holocaust Resource Center
of Minneapolis
8200 West 33rd Street
Minneapolis, MN 55426

Holocaust Resource Center
Bureau of Jewish Education
441 East Avenue
Rochester, NY 14607

Holocaust Studies Center
The Bronx High School
of Science
75 West 205th Street
Bronx, NY 10468

Jewish Holocaust Museum
and Research Center
13 Selwyn Street
Elsternwick
Victoria 3185, Australia

Leo Baeck Institute
129 East 73rd Street
New York, NY 10021

A Living Memorial to the Holocaust-
Museum of Jewish Heritage
342 Madison Avenue, Suite 706
New York, NY 10173

Martyrs Memorial and Museum
of the Holocaust of the
Jewish Federation Council
6505 Wilshire Boulevard
Los Angeles, CA 90048

Joseph Meyerhoff Library
Baltimore Hebrew University
5800 Park Heights Avenue
Baltimore, MD 21215

The Montreal Holocaust
Memorial Centre
5151 Cote Street, Catherine Road
Montreal, Quebec
Canada H3W 1M6

Oregon Holocaust Resource Center
2900 SW Peaceful Lane
Portland, OR 97201

Rhode Island Holocaust
Memorial Museum
JCC of Rhode Island
401 Elmgrove Avenue
Providence, RI 02906

Rockland Center for
Holocaust Studies, Inc.
17 South Madison Avenue
Spring Valley, NY 10977

Simon Wiesenthal Center
9760 West Pico Boulevard
Los Angeles, CA 90035

Saint Louis Center for
Holocaust Studies
12 Millstone Campus Drive
Saint Louis, MO 63146

Sonoma State University
Holocaust Studies Center
Alliance for the Study of
The Holocaust
Rohnert Park, CA 94928

Tampa Bay Holocaust Memorial
Museum and Educational Center
5001 113th Street (Duhme Road)
Saint Petersburg, FL 33708

United States Holocaust
Memorial Museum
100 Raoul Wallenberg Place, SW
(15th Street & Independence Avenue)
Washington, DC 20024

Vancouver Holocaust Centre
for Education and Remembrance
950 West 41st Avenue
Vancouver, British Columbia
Canada V5Z 2N7

The Vanderbilt University
Holocaust Art Collection
Vanderbilt University
402 Sarratt Student Center
Nashville, TN 37240

Yad Vashem—The Holocaust
Martyrs' and Heroes'
Remembrance Authority
P. O. Box 3477
Jerusalem, Israel 91034

Zachor Holocaust Center
1753 Peachtree Road, NE
Atlanta, GA 30309

This information was provided by the Association of Holocaust Organizations, Holocaust Resource Center and Archives, Queensborough Community College, Bayside, New York. For additional locations and further details, including hours of operation and telephone numbers, you may call them at 718-225-1617.

Notes

1. Martin Luther, *Against the Jews*.
2. Irvin J Borowsky, American Interfaith Institute, 401 N. Broad St., Philadelphia, PA 19108.
3. Konrad Heiden, *Der Fuehrer* (Boston: Houghton-Mifflin Co., 1944), pp. 773-74.
4. Adolf Hitler, *Mein Kampf*, p. 113.
5. Ibid., pp. 324-25.
6. William L. Shirer, *The Rise and Fall of the Third Reich* (New York: Simon and Schuster, 1960), p. 239.
7. *Christians Must*, vol. 4, p. 260.
8. *The Talmud: Pesachim* 54b; *Midrash Tehilim* 9:2. See *Zohar Chadash*, Bereishit, 8a.
9. *The Talmud: Midrash Tehilim* 45:3; cf. *Besha'ah Shehikdimu*-5672, vol I: 551, relating this to the principle (*Midrash Tehelim* 22:4; *Zohar* 11:46a) that the darkest moments of the night are immediately before daybreak. For this analogy see also the comment by R. Elijah, the Vilna Gaon, cited in *Even Shelemah*, ch. 11:5.
10. *Sotah* 49b.
11. *Sanhedrin* 97a; *Shir Rabba* 2:29.
12. *Sanhedrin* 98a.
13. *Bereishit Rabba* 42:4. Note *Pesikta Rabaty* 37:2 (ed. Friedmann, ch. 36).
14. *Sanhedrin* 98b.
15. Text of Anti-Missionary Law.
16. *Toward Tradition Perspectives*, Fall 1994.
17. Michael J. Pragai, *Faith and Fulfillment* (London: Vallentine, Mitchel and Co., Ltd., 1985), p.57.
18. *Prince and Prophet*, p. 9.
19. Raphael Patai, ed., *Encyclopedia of Zionism and Israel* (New York: Herzl Press / McCraw Hill, 1971).
20. Pragai, *Faith and Fulfillment*, p. 45.
21. Ibid., p. 60.
22. Claude Duvernoy, *The Prince and the Prophet*, p.48.
23. Ibid., p. 50.
24. Pragai, *Faith and Fulfillment*, p. 82.
25. Ibid., p. 100.
26. Ibid., pp. 84,86

27. Ibid., p. 88.

28. Ibid., p. 113.

29. *The International Jew*, 1:33, 34.

30. Ibid., 1:37, 63.

31. Ibid., 1:39, 41, 71.

32. Ibid., 1:160-62; 4:68, 71-72.

33. Ibid., l:63.

34. Cecil Roth, *The Jewish Contribution to Civilization*, pp. 214-15.

35. Taken from a CNN transcript of an "Early Edition" interview, May 29, 1995.

36. "Callling Our Nation," *Aryan Nations*, no. 48, pp. 15, 16.

37. Ibid.

38. Mullins, p. 23.

39. *Response*, August 1985, Simon Wiesenthel Center, Los Angeles, CA, p.5.

40. *Racial and National Identity*, pp. 3-4.

41. Ibid., pp. 11-12.

42. Ibid., pp. 6-7.

43. Ibid., p. 18.

44. "White Supremists See Computers as Revolutionary Key," Associated Press, March 3, 1985.

45. Associated Press report, March 3, 1985.

46. "Calling Our Nation," no. 48.

47. Robert Morey, *The Islamic Invasion*, (Eugene, OR: Harvest House, 1992), p. 168.

48. Ibid., p. 173.

49. Harold Brackman, Ph.D., *Ministry of Lies: The Truth Behind the nations of Islam's "The Secret Relationship* Between Blacks and Jews" (New York: Four Walls, Eight Windows, 1994), p. 116.

50. Ibid.

51. Bediuzzam Said Nursi, *The Muslim-Christian Alliance* (Istanbul: Nisan, 1992), p. 13.

52. Ibid., pp. 4, 5.

53. Morey, *Islamic Invasion*, p. 22.

54. Tamim Al-Adnani, Kansas, 1988.

55. Abdulla Azzam, at the First Conference of Jihad, Brooklyn, New York, 1989.

56. Fayiz Azzam, Atlanta, Georgia, 1990.

57. Omar Abdul Rahman, Detroit, Michigan, 1991.

58. Siddiq Ali, New Jersey, 1992.

59. Clement Rodney Hampton-El, New York, 1988.

60. Kenneth R. Timmerman, *In Their Own Words* (Los Angeles: Simon Weisenthal Center, 1994), p. 13.

61. Ibid., p. 15.

62. Walid Phares, World Lebanese Organization, P.O. Box 331195, Miami, FL 33233-1195.

63. *Middle East Intelligence Digest*, February 1994.

64. *The Boston Herald*, Thursday, June 16, 1994.

65. *Kansas City Star*, July 5, 1994.

66. *Commentary Magazine*, September 1994.

67. *Pagan America*, pp. 16-17.

68. Ibid., p. 110.

69. Quoted from Feder, *Pagan America*, pp. 70-71.

70. *The Washington Post*, June 26, 1994.

71. Michael Ledeen, "Should Jews Fear the Religious Right?" *Moment Magazine*, October 1994.

Bibliography

A Cup of Trembling, Dave Hunt (Eugene, Oregon: Harvest House Publishers, 1995).

A Jewish Conservative Looks at Pagan America, Don Feder (Louisiana: Huntington House Publishers, 1993).

Der Fuehrer, Konrad Heiden (Boston: Houghton Mifflin Company, 1944).

Encyclopedia Judaica Volume 13 (Jerusalem: Keter Publishing House Jerusalem Ltd., 1972).

Faith and Fulfilment: Christians and the Return of the Promised Land, Michael J. Pragai (London: Vallentine, Mitchell and Company Limited, 1985).

Encyclopedia Judaica (Jerusalem: Keter Publishing House Jerusalem Ltd., 1972).

Encyclopedia of Zionism and Israel, Edited by Raphael Pata (New York: Herzl Press/McGraw-Hill, 1971).

The Hebrew Impact on Western Civilisation, Dagobert D. Runes (New York: Philosophical Library, Inc., 1951).

The Hiding Place, Corrie ten Boom with John and Elizabeth Sherrill (Connecticut: Chosen Books, 1971).

The History of Anti-Semitism, Leon Poliakov.

The International Jew, (Dearborn: Dearborn Independent, 1920-22).

In Their Own Words, Kenneth R. Timmerman (Los Angeles: Simon Wiesenthal Center, 1994).

The Islamic Invasion, Robert Morey (Eugene, Oregon: Harvest House Publishers, 1992).

Israel My Glory, Vol. 51, No. 2 (Bellmawr, NJ: The Friends of Israel Gospel Ministry, Inc., 1993).

It Is No Dream, Elwood McQuaid (Bellmawr, NJ: The Friends of Israel Gospel Ministry, Inc., 1978).

Jesus is Coming, William Blackstone (Chicago: Moody Bible Institute, 1908).

The Jewish Almanac, Richard Siegel and Carl Rheins (New York: Bantam Books, Inc., 1980).

The Jewish Contribution to Civilization, Cecil Roth (London: Macmillan and Co., Limited, 1938).

"Jihad In America." Executive Producer and Correspondent: Steven Emerson. Produced by SAE Productions for PBS.

The Kingdom of the Cults, Walter Martin (Minneapolis: Bethany Books, 1985).

Mein Kampf, Adolf Hitler, translated by Ralph Manheim (Boston: The Houghton Mifflin Company, 1971).

Ministry of Lies: The Truth Behind the Nation of Islam's "The Secret Relationship Between Blacks and Jews." Harold Brackman, Ph. D. (NewYork: Four Walls Eight Windows, 1994).

Mashiach: Principle of Mashiach and the Messianic Era in Jewish Law and Tradition, Immanuel Schocket (New York and Ontario: S.I.E, 1991).

Muslim-Christian Alliance. Said Nursi Bediuzzaman

Myths and Facts, Mitchell G. Bard and Joel Himelfarb (Washington: Near East Report, 1984, 1988,1992).

The Path of The Righteous: Gentile Rescuers of Jews of the Holocaust, Mordecai Paldiel (Hoboken, New Jersey: KTAV Publishing House, Inc., 1993).

The Prince and the Prophet, Claude Duvernoy (Jerusalem: Claude Duvernoy, 1979).

The Prophecy Knowledge Handbook, John F. Walvoord (Wheaton, Illinois: Victor Books a division of Scripture Press Publications, Inc., 1990).

Protocols of the Learned Elders of Zion, translation by Victor E. Marsden (Ontario: Canadian Publications).

Racial and National Identity, Rev. William P. Gale (California: Ministry of Christ Church).

The Rise and Fall of the Third Reich, William L. Shirer (New York: Simon and Schuster, 1960).

The Secret Holocaust, Eustace Mullins (Idaho: Aryan Nations, 1984).

The Twentieth Century in Europe, Kenneth Scott Latourette (Grand Rapids: Zondervan Publishing House, 1961).

Other Good
Harvest House Reading

MY SAVIOR, MY FRIEND
by *Kay Arthur*

In 366 daily readings, Kay Arthur uncovers beautiful facets of John's Gospel, which has been called the most precious jewel of the Word of God. Much more than simply getting by, John wrote so that we might have life in Jesus' name. To know Jesus as Savior and Friend is to have life—here, now, eternal, and abundant!

THE INTERNATIONAL INDUCTIVE STUDY BIBLE
Now available in NASB and NIV

The first of its kind in Bible-publishing history, *The International Inductive Study Bible* teaches you how to unearth the treasures of God's Word for yourself. It Includes study helps, four-color maps and charts, and a concordance.

NEXT YEAR IN JERUSALEM
by *Teddy Kolleck,*
photographs by *Max Moshe* and *Hill Jacoby*

This beautiful full-color book from Jerusalem's long-time mayor explores the nooks and crannies of the Old City—and the hearts of those who have lived within its shadow. Every page reflects the history, the traditions, and the beauty of this unique world city.

JERUSALEM: THE CITY OF GOD
by *Ellen Gunderson Traylor*

Over 3000 years of history, the city's violence and peace, safety and vulnerability, honor and betrayal are woven into the lives of unforgettable characters. Its moving narrative will inspire Christians to a deeper understanding of their heritage and move them to passion for the God of Israel and Jesus the Messiah.